The Tabernacle's Typical Teaching

Algernon J Pollock

Scripture Truth Publications

Hardback edition first published c1921 by The Northern Counties Bible and Tract Depot, 63a, Blackett Street, Newcastle-on-Tyne (London Agents: The Central Bible Truth Depôt, 5, Rose Street, Paternoster Square, London, E.C.4.)
Reprinted 1921 by Pickering & Inglis, London.
Second edition 1945 by The Central Bible Truth Depôt, 11, Little Britain, London, E.C.1.
Third edition c1967 by The Central Bible Truth Depôt, 50, Grays Inn Road, London, W.C.1.
Re-typeset and transferred to Digital Printing 2009
ISBN: 978-0-901860-65-1 (paperback)
Copyright © 1921 The Northern Counties Bible and Tract Depôt and 2009 Scripture Truth Publications in this edition

Scripture quotations are taken from The Authorized (King James) Version. Rights in the Authorized Version are vested in the Crown. Reproduced by permission of the Crown's patentee, Cambridge University Press.

Illustrations © 2009 Arthur J Duff
Cover photograph ©iStockphoto.com/ratluk

Published by Scripture Truth Publications
31-33 Glover Street, Crewe, Cheshire, CW1 3LD

Scripture Truth is an imprint of Central Bible Hammond Trust, a charitable trust

Typesetting by John Rice
Printed and bound by Lightning Source

Preface to 2009 Edition

This edition contains the re-typeset text of the third edition. In checking the text, reference has also been made to previous editions.

To assist the twenty-first century reader, minor changes in presentation have been made. The use of quotation (speech) marks has been updated. Scriptural references have been expanded to provide the full title of the book and the format has been standardized to facilitate ease of lookup. Quotations have been attributed where possible. Rather than amend the main text, notes on topics such as weights, measures and values have been included in an appendix.

The first edition was illustrated by photographs of a series of paintings by James Green. Bertram Adkins provided illustrations for subsequent editions. For this edition, a new set of illustrations have been drawn by Arthur Duff.

The author wrote in a postscript to the first edition:

> "The reward of this modest volume will be if it whets the appetite of the reader, leading him to desire to know more of these wondrous subjects. The theme is delightful indeed as it leads the heart into contact with Christ, subduing it by a deepening sense of the meaning of the death of Christ, leading out at the same time the affections of the heart to Him to Whom the believer owes everything for time and eternity."

The publishers commend this book to you. As you read, may your appreciation grow of the wonder of the One who is indeed the Tabernacle's true Theme.

John Rice

Contents

LIST OF ILLUSTRATIONS

PAGE

Foreword

There are two ways of approach to this subject. There is that of the Modernist, who sees in the teaching concerning the Tabernacle in the wilderness nothing more than a dry recital of the meaningless ritual of the worship of a primitive race long centuries ago. For instance, a Professor of a Theological College wrote:—

"What value for spiritual life can we find in the minute liturgical and ceremonial details of the Tabernacle and its service?" (Peake's Commentary, p. 5).

On the other hand, the well-known writer of helpful Christian literature, the late Sir Robert Anderson, put upon record how the opening up of the spiritual meaning of the Jewish ceremonial law convinced him of the wonderful inspiration of Scripture, and was the means of his taking his stand as a definite Christian.

We wonder what kind of spiritual myopia affected the vision of this modernist Professor when he read the Epistle to the Hebrews. There Moses is contrasted with Christ. Aaron is contrasted with Christ. That mysterious figure, Melchizedek, is contrasted with Christ. The ineffectual sacrifices on Jewish altars are contrasted with the one great, atoning, efficacious sacrifice of Christ. Scripture itself describes these Old Testament types as

"The example and shadow of heavenly things" (Hebrews 8:5).

"The patterns of things in the heavens" (Hebrews 9:23).

"A shadow of good things to come" (Hebrews 10:1).

"Every whit of it uttereth His glory" (Psalm 29:9, AV margin).

What kind of spectacles did the Professor wear when he read such plain statements as these? We can only come to the conclusion that he failed to see the beauty of the types, because he did not know the glory of the Antitype, even of our Lord Jesus Christ. Scripture compresses it into one word:—

"A shadow of things to come; but the body [or Substance in contrast to the shadow] is of Christ" (Colossians 2:17).

CHRIST then is our happy theme—His Deity, Manhood, atoning death, finished work, resurrection, the blessings that flow in rich streams from Him to His people in their association with Him.

Less than two chapters (Genesis 1 and 2) suffice to tell us of the mighty work of creation. Indeed one short verse gives us in nine words the record, "The worlds were framed by the word of God" (Hebrews 11:3). But no less than thirteen chapters in Exodus alone are taken up with instructions as to the Tabernacle and its services. Indeed, we may say a large part of the teaching and instructions of the Pentateuch stands mainly in relation to the

Tabernacle. This shows the great importance of our theme.

Someone has well described the Tabernacle as "a prophecy in linen, silver, and gold". It is instinct with deep spiritual meaning. It is fragrant of Christ. It is a striking testimony to the fullness and inspiration of the word of God. Its teaching is one of the richest mines of purest gold in the whole Bible.

Creation was necessary to afford a platform on which God could carry out His plan. The shadows of that scheme are given us in the Tabernacle. The earth in which we live is but the scaffolding for the erection of the building of God for eternity. The Sabbath is a shadow of God being all in all throughout eternity. The scaffolding will be taken down one day. The building of God will arise majestic and eternal to God's glory and praise. God will yet rest in the complacency of His love, dwelling among His people, in a scene where there will be no tears, pain, sorrow or death.

NOTE

In going over the details of the types and shadows the same truths are emphasized over and over again. So the reader must be prepared for a good deal of repetition in the following pages. This is unavoidable in dealing with such a subject. On the other hand, one cannot go into every small detail, but be content with a more or less general survey of this intensely interesting portion of God's Word. The writer has felt the repetition very precious to his own soul, and the continual affirmation of foundation truths as to our Lord's Deity, Manhood, earthly life, atoning death, and glorious resurrection, etc., very necessary and helpful.

An archbishop in an address to his clergy in Convocation said, "We often forget what all teachers should remember, the value of frequent repetition of what is of fundamental importance, and the danger of so taking for granted what is fundamental that in the result we never teach it at all." Wise and weighty words!

Chapter 1:
The Collection of Materials for the Construction of the Tabernacle, and their Typical Meaning

READ **EXODUS 25:1-9**

Not fewer than 603,550 males, Israelites of twenty years old and upward, paid the atonement money that was taken of the children of Israel in the wilderness, when God numbered His people. This number did not include the tribe of Levi (see Numbers 1:46-47), which was specially set aside for the service of the Tabernacle. From this we gather that roughly speaking some three million souls must have come out of Egypt, when God "with a mighty hand, and with an outstretched arm" delivered His people from the bitter bondage of Pharaoh.

What a stirring tale it is, a tribute to God's mighty power and abounding mercy. Sheltered by the blood of the Passover night, saved by power as God's mighty hand brought them through the Red Sea, this host of erstwhile slaves found themselves God's redeemed people on the wilderness side of the Red Sea, on the opposite shore of which lay Egypt, the land of their bitter bondage.

What warrant, we may ask, have we for applying this incident of the Passover to Christ?

The modernist Professor would say we had none. Scripture says: "CHRIST, our Passover, is sacrificed for us" (1 Corinthians 5:7). "All these things happened unto them for ensamples [or types]: and they are written for our admonition, upon whom the ends of the world are come" (1 Corinthians 10:11). "Whatsoever things were written aforetime were written for our learning, that we through patience and comfort of the Scriptures might have hope" (Romans 15:4).

The Passover is the foundation of the spiritual history of Israel as a nation. By it God declared that redemption by blood is the one and only foundation of His dealings with men. On this foundation God announced His good pleasure to dwell among His people. To this end He instructed Moses as to the construction of the Tabernacle, the order of the Sacrifices, the Service of the priests, the work of the Levites, and the conduct of a people thus brought into relationship with Himself. If *God Himself* instructed Moses as to these details, how can it be said that they are the dry recital of a ritualistic worship of a primitive race with no voice to us to-day?

The Tabernacle was divided into two compartments. The first and larger was where the priests performed their sacred offices. It was called the Holy Place, or the Sanctuary. The inner and smaller compartment was called the Holiest of All. It was where the glory of God dwelt upon the Mercy Seat.

For its size the Tabernacle was perhaps the most expensive structure that has ever been. Over £160,000 of gold and over £34,000 of silver [1], besides quantities of linen, precious stones, rare spices, oil, blue, purple, scarlet dyes, etc., were used in its construction. The weight of the silver has been computed at 4 tons. This small building, its total length about 54 feet, its breadth about 16 feet, was valued at about £200,000. This is at a low computation of the value of gold. To-day it would be estimated at a much higher figure. The Court of the Tabernacle was roughly 180 feet by 90 feet.

When we reflect who furnished the materials our astonishment deepens. The Israelites had just escaped from bitter bondage. Their lot had been rigorous. "Bricks without straw" had plumbed the depths of the misery of sweated labour. Yet these were the people who so willingly offered of their substance that Moses had to restrain their flood of generosity.

We read of the offerers that "every one whose heart stirred him up, and every one whom his spirit made willing" (Exodus 35:21) gladly contributed to the work of the Lord. Men and women brought their bracelets, earrings, rings, tablets, and jewels of gold; the "wise-hearted" women spun linen and goats' hair; the rulers brought precious stones, spices and oil.

What a lesson for us. "He which soweth sparingly shall reap also sparingly; and he which soweth bountifully shall reap also bountifully ... God loveth a cheerful giver" (2 Corinthians 9:6-7). The widow, who cast in her two mites—all her living—into the Treasury of the Temple, when that system was drawing to a close, and had Ichabod, "the glory hath departed", written upon it, might well encourage us at the end of this dispensation to serve the Lord with might and main. He will be no man's debtor, nor is He unrighteous to forget the work and labour of love done in His name.

In seeking to give the typical significance of the various articles in the construction of the Tabernacle, the ordering of the Sacrifices, etc., it is well to remember that we cannot dogmatize, but that we offer our explanations to the spiritual judgment of the reader. Many things in Scripture we can, and must, be dogmatic about—doctrines for instance, which are vital and fundamental, such as the Deity, Manhood, atoning work and resurrection of our Lord Jesus Christ, the presence and work of God's Holy Spirit, the Church of God, her origin, blessings and destiny, the calling and ultimate blessing of Israel, God's earthly people. These truths are directly affirmed in Scripture.

And even in the types there are things we can be dogmatic about. The Passover is typical of Christ's atoning death on the cross. Our warrant for this is the Scripture: "CHRIST, *our Passover*, is sacrificed for us" (1 Corinthians 5:7). Again, *the Mercy Seat* is typical of Christ in His atoning death, enabling God in all His holiness to meet and bless the vilest sinner. Our warrant for this is found in the Scripture: "God hath set forth [*Christ*] to be a propitiation [literally, *a Mercy Seat*] through faith in His blood" (Romans 3:25).

Bearing all this in mind let us proceed with our explanations: —

Gold, typical of Deity when in reference to Christ; of Divine righteousness when seen in relation to men. In Exodus whenever gold is typical of Deity, it is always *"pure gold"*: when it typifies Divine righteousness, the word gold is employed without the adjective "pure".

Silver, typical of redemption. The half shekel of silver, worth about 1s. 1½d. [2], demanded of the males from twenty years and upward when Israel was numbered, is described as "atonement money" (Exodus 30:16).

Brass, typical of atonement in the aspect of the judgment of God being met at the cross of Christ in relation to *man's responsibility*. As a matter of fact the word, "brass", as employed in Scripture, should rightly be translated *copper*. Brass is an alloy of copper and zinc or spelter, and is not so fire-resisting as copper. Keeping this in mind to prevent confusion, we will follow the phraseology employed in our Authorized Version, and speak of the Brazen Altar, the Brazen Laver.

Blue, typical of what is heavenly. The Hindustani name for heaven is simply their word for *blue*. It is the colour of the cloudless sky.

Purple, typical of the glory of Christ as King of kings and Lord of lords. An Emperor is strictly a King of kings. Purple was the distinctive colour used by the Roman Emperors. "To don the purple" meant to ascend the Imperial throne.

Scarlet, typical of the glory of Christ as King of Israel. Scarlet is the kingly colour. In mockery of our Lord's claim to be the King of Israel the soldiers put on Him "a scarlet robe" (Matthew 27:28).

Fine Linen, typical of the spotless, pure and holy human-ity of our Lord; or of that, which is the product of the Holy Spirit of God in the lives of believers. "The fine linen is the righteousness of saints" (Revelation 19:8).

Goats' Hair, typical of Christ as Prophet. Zechariah 13:4-5 shows that a rough or hairy garment was the mark of a prophet. When the sick Ahaziah enquired what sort of man it was, who met his messengers, they replied that "he was an hairy man [*that is, that he wore an hairy garment*], and girt with a girdle of leather about his loins" (2 Kings 1:8). The King immediately recognized the description as that of Elijah the prophet. John, the Baptist, too, is described as having "raiment of camel's hair, and a leathern girdle about his loins" (Matthew 3:4).

Ram's Skins Dyed Red, typical of Christ's devotedness to God's glory even to death. The "ram" is called "the ram of ... consecration" (Exodus 29:26). "Dyed red" signified the length to which consecration can go, even to death.

Badgers' Skins, typical of Christ as seen by the world. These formed the outward covering of the Tabernacle. Illustrates Isaiah 53:2: "He hath no form nor comeliness; and when we shall see Him, there is no beauty that we should desire Him."

Shittim Wood, typical of the humanity of our Lord, and also of the believer as seen in the boards of the Tabernacle.

Oil, typical of God's Holy Spirit. The Holy Spirit is called in the New Testament "the Anointing" (1 John 2:27). Kings, prophets and priests were anointed with oil in Old Testament times.

Spices, typical of the fragrance of Christ before God.

Onyx and Precious Stones, typical of the preciousness of believers to God, the outcome of their relations to Christ.

Sanctuary, typical of God's dwelling place among His people, a Holy Place set apart for God's pleasure. "Let them make me a Sanctuary; that I may dwell among them" (Exodus 25:8).

"According to the Pattern"—Human mind and imagination are not left to work out what is suitable to God. Moses was called up to the top of Mount Sinai. The elders of Israel saw him disappear in the glory of the Lord, like a

devouring fire on the top of the Mount. There he was instructed by God Himself, and exhorted, "Look that thou make them [*the various parts of the Tabernacle*] after their pattern, which was shewed thee in the Mount" (Exodus 25:40).

Seeing all these details have been designed by God Himself in order to teach His people lessons of heavenly things, these types and shadows become intensely interesting, and their study not to be neglected without real loss to the soul.

Just as refraction breaks up colourless light into its seven prismatic colours, so the types break up, as it were, the great truths concerning Christ—His Deity, Manhood, atoning work, the blessing and standing of His people—into instructive details. And as we learn these details, and one aspect after another is brought before us, one detail fitting into another, gradually the right appreciation of the whole is formed in our souls, till the truth is woven into the very fibre of our spiritual being, affecting us for God's glory. The writer can never be sufficiently thankful for the wonderful teaching as to the Person and death of Christ to be learned from the types, teaching which cannot be obtained elsewhere.

Chapter 2:
The Significance of Numbers in the Construction and Service of the Tabernacle

THE SIGNIFICANCE OF THE NUMBER THREE

Three is the number bespeaking abundant testimony. "In the mouth of two or three witnesses every word may be established" (Matthew 18:16). It speaks first of all of Divine testimony in all its stability and permanence as seen in the testimony of Father, Son and Holy Spirit.

THREE PERSONS WERE REPRESENTED IN THE TABERNACLE:—

1. GOD—His presence filled the Holy of Holies, dwelling upon the Mercy Seat, the place where He can righteously meet the vilest sinner without abating one iota of the claims of His holiness.

2. CHRIST, typified as to His Deity, Manhood and atoning death as seen in the Ark and Mercy Seat.

3. THE HOLY SPIRIT—typified in the *light* of the Golden Candlestick, and in the anointing Oil.

THREE SECTIONS COMPOSED THE TABERNACLE:—

1. The Holiest of All, the Holy of Holies.

2. The Holy Place, or Sanctuary.

3. The Court of the Tabernacle.

THREE METALS ENTERED IN THE CONSTRUCTION OF THE TABERNACLE:—

1. *Gold*—typifying the Deity of our Lord Jesus Christ, and also of Divine righteousness as seen in the Mercy Seat.

2. *Silver*—typifying redemption as seen in the half shekel of silver being called "atonement money".

3. *Brass*—typifying the death of Christ as meeting *man's responsibility* towards God. This is seen in the Brazen Altar, the one and only approach to God.

THREE LIQUIDS WERE EMPLOYED IN THE SERVICE OF THE TABERNACLE:—

These were blood, water, oil, the *three* witnesses referred to in 1 John 5:8, "And there are *three* that bear witness in earth, the Spirit [*typified in the oil*], and the water [*the word of God*], and the blood [*atonement*]: and these *three* agree in one."

1. *Blood* witnesses to the death of Christ, as meeting the question of *guilt*.

2. *Water* witnesses to the death of Christ, as meeting the question of *state*—"BORN of *water*, and of the *Spirit*" (John 3:5).

3. *Oil*, typifies the Holy Spirit of God, the Divine Agent, whereby man can be born again, of which John 3:5 affirms the necessity, if we have to do with God.

These will be explained in greater detail later on.

Three things were In the Holiest of All:—

1. *The Ark.*

2   *The Mercy Seat.*

3. *The Cherubims* "beaten out of *one* piece" of gold (Exodus 37:7).

Three things were in the Holy Place:—

1. *The Table of Shewbread*, typifying Christ, the Food of His people.

2. *The Golden Candlestick*, Christ the light of His people.

3. *The Golden Altar*, the place of worship and intercession.

Three things were in the Court of the Tabernacle:—

1. *The Gate of the Court*, typifying Christ, who said, "I Am The Way" (John 14:6).

2. *The Brazen Altar*, typifying the necessity of an atoning sacrifice if sinners are to be blessed.

3. *The Brazen Laver* filled with *water*, typifying the cleansing quality of the Word of God applied to the worshipper, emphasizing that holiness is necessary for those who would approach God for Sanctuary service.

Three entrances marked the Tabernacle:—

1. *The Gate of the Court*, the entrance for the *sinner*.

2. *The Hanging for the Door of the Tent*, that is the entrance to the Holy Place for the priest.

3. *The Vail*, that formed the entrance from the Holy Place into the Holiest of All, the entrance for the *High Priest* on the Great Day of Atonement.

THREE KINDS OF SACRIFICES WERE ENUMERATED,

They all spoke of Christ as the great Sacrifice for sin:—

1. *Of the herd*—a bullock.

2. *Of the flock*—a sheep, or goat.

3. *Of fowls*—turtle doves, or young pigeons.

THREE SONS OF LEVI

in the persons of their descendants carried out the Levitical service of the Tabernacle:—

1. *The Sons of Merari* (3200) carried the boards, bars, pillars, sockets, pins, etc.

2. *The Sons of Gershon* (2630) carried the curtains, the hanging of the Court, etc.

3. *The Sons of Kohath* (2750) carried the Holy Vessels. (See Numbers 4.)

THREE COLOURS WERE EMPLOYED IN THE CURTAINS:—

1. *Blue*, the heavenly colour, typifying Christ the Heavenly Man.

2. *Purple*, the colour of the Emperor, typifying Christ the King of kings and Lord of lords, who will reign universally.

3. *Scarlet*, the kingly colour, typifying Christ King of Israel.

THREE CLASSES COMPOSED THE NATION:—

1. *"The children of Israel"*—"the common people"—"the people".

2. *The Levites.*

3. *The Priests.*

"The common people" (Leviticus 4:27) stood in contrast to the *sacred* or set-apart classes, the Levites and Priests.

Yet their relation to Jehovah called for holiness of ways before Him.

The Levites attended to the taking down, and putting up, of the Tabernacle, and its transport as it journeyed from place to place.

The Priests attended to the Sacrifices, Golden Candlestick, Shewbread Table, Golden Altar of Incense, etc.

Let it be clearly understood that believers in this dispensation stand for all three classes. In our domestic, business, and everyday life we are "common people", yet belonging to the House of God demands holiness of walk on our part. As serving the Lord we are performing what answers to the service of the Levites. Finally, *all* believers are priests. The Apostle Peter, addressing believers, wrote, "Ye ... are ... an holy priesthood, to offer up spiritual sacrifices, acceptable to God by Jesus Christ" (1 Peter 2:5); whilst the Apostle John tells us that God "hath made us kings and priests [*literally, a kingdom of priests*] unto God and His Father" (Revelation 1:6). All believers are priests to God, and have "boldness to enter into the Holiest by the blood of Jesus" (Hebrews 10:19).

THE SIGNIFICANCE OF THE NUMBER FOUR

Four is the number symbolizing what is universal or worldwide. We speak of "the *four* winds" (Ezekiel 37:9); of "the *four* corners of the earth" (Isaiah 11:12).

FOUR CURTAINS, OR COVERINGS OF THE TABERNACLE,

set forth Christ in His universal relation to men:—

1. *Curtains of fine twined linen, and blue and purple and scarlet with cherubims of cunning work* set forth the *four* glories of the Son of God:—

a. *Blue* setting forth Christ as the One from Heaven;

b. *Purple*, symbolizing His glory as King of kings and Lord of lords, the Son of Man;

c. *Scarlet*, typical of His glory as King of Israel;

d. *Cherubims* worked in the curtains set forth Christ in His judicial character in His relation to Heaven and earth, whether in grace or judgment.

2. *Goats' Hair Curtains* set forth Christ in His prophetic office, as we have seen.

3. *Rams' Skins dyed red* set forth Christ's devotedness to God, obedience to His will, the colour red signifying that His obedience led to death itself.

4. *Badgers' Skins* which were *outside* set forth what Christ was in the eyes of the natural man, no beauty in Him that He should be desired. In contrast, the beautiful curtains *inside* met the eyes of the priests as they ministered in the Sanctuary.

Foursquare was the Brazen Altar,

symbolizing that the atoning death of Christ is not merely for the few, the elect, but that "Christ ... gave Himself a Ransom for ALL" (1 Timothy 2:5-6). "God so loved THE WORLD, that He gave His only begotten Son, that WHOSOEVER believeth in Him should not perish, but have everlasting life" (John 3:16). The Altar *four*square invites from the *four* quarters of the earth. No sinner but is welcome to the pardoning grace of God.

Four horns on the Altar

intensifies the foregoing, for the horns symbolize the whole strength of the Altar.

FOURSQUARE WAS THE GOLDEN ALTAR OF INCENSE,

and *four* were the number of its horns, showing that all, who come by the way of the Brazen Altar, are welcome to the Golden Altar of Incense. That is to say that all, who are saved, are fitted to be worshippers. But all alas! do not come by the way of the Brazen Altar. So we find that while the Brazen Altar had the ample measurement of *five* cubits in length and *five* in breadth (*four*square), and *three* cubits high, the Golden Altar of Incense (typical of worship and intercession) is but *one* cubit in length, and *one* cubit in breadth ("*four*square shall it be" (Exodus 30:2)), and *two* cubits high, thus bringing out the truth that whilst the invitation goes out to all, all do not respond.

FOUR PILLARS UPHELD THE HANGING OF THE GATE OF THE COURT

of the Tabernacle, symbolical of the *universal* presentation of the Gospel of the grace of God. This was the only entrance into the sacred enclosure, and seems to say, "Go ye into *all* the world, and preach the Gospel to *every* creature" (Mark 16:15).

FOUR WAS THE NUMBER OF THE "PRINCIPAL SPICES" (EXODUS 30:23),

which with oil compounded "the holy anointing oil". The anointing of the Tabernacle, of its Sacred Vessels, of its High Priests and priests, teaches us that God had in view the presentation of Himself as ready to bless *universally*, and that on the ground of what Christ was to Him in all His fragrance as THE ANOINTED ONE, for that is the meaning of the word, *Messiah*, in the Hebrew, and its equivalent, *Christ*, in the Greek.

The first of the spices mentioned was myrrh. To obtain its sweetness it had to be bruised. So Christ was "bruised for our iniquities" (Isaiah 53:5), and made atonement for our sin. In life and death how fragrant was He to the Father, who sent Him. It is thus that the Holy Spirit (typified by the oil) can present Him to God in all that ineffable delight that He ever gave to the heart of God.

> *"Love that on death's dark vale,*
> *Its sweetest odours spread,*
> *Where sin o'er all seemed to prevail,*
> *Redemption's glory shed."*

FOUR WAS THE NUMBER OF THE "SWEET SPICES" (EXODUS 30:34).

Tempered together they made a perfume pure and holy, "the pure incense of sweet spices" (Exodus 37:29), which, beaten "very small", was to be put before the Testimony in the Tabernacle of the Congregation. Both this and the holy anointing oil remind us of the *four*fold presentation of Christ in the *four* Gospels—Matthew setting forth Christ in His kingly character, "the Lion of the Tribe of Judah"; Mark presenting Him as the obedient Servant of God in lowly grace; Luke, as the Man, Christ Jesus; John portraying Him in His own proper Person, the Son of the Father, the Eternal Word, which became flesh. Each of these four Gospels narrates the death of our Lord. What a fragrant presentation of our Lord in life and in death.

The holy anointing oil was to be poured on no man's flesh. The sacred perfume was not to be made for private consumption on pain of death, thus showing that the blessed Lord stands *alone* in His life and death, and in their wonderful results, which are to bring blessing to a redeemed universe.

THE SIGNIFICANCE OF THE NUMBER FIVE AND ITS MULTIPLES

Five is the number speaking of human responsibility. Its multiples only intensify the thought.

It is the figure with its multiple *ten* that is stamped on the human frame. *Five* fingers on each hand, *ten* in all, speaks of human responsibility in *work*; *five* toes on each foot, *ten* in all, our responsibility in *walk*; the *five* senses—seeing, hearing, smelling, tasting, feeling—represent the whole range of human receptiveness in its responsibility to God.

To this may be added the *Ten* Commandments, which written upon two tables of stone, *five* on each, summarize human responsibility whether Godward or manward.

FIVE CUBITS WAS THE LENGTH, FIVE CUBITS THE BREADTH OF THE BRAZEN ALTAR.

They symbolize that sacrifice must meet human responsibility, if man is to be blessed.

Ten cubits high were the boards of the Tabernacle, typifying man in his responsibility before God. Later we shall show how this was met.

Twenty was the number of the boards on the south side of the Tabernacle; *twenty* boards on the north side; *forty* sockets of silver provided for the south side; *forty* sockets for the north side; *one hundred* sockets of silver in all provided for the boards, and the pillars, and the hanging of the Vail. (See Exodus 38:27.)

FIVE BARS BOUND THE TWENTY BOARDS INTO ONE COMPACT STRUCTURE.

FIVE PILLARS AND FIVE SOCKETS OF BRASS MARKED THE ENTRANCE TO THE HOLY PLACE.

Ten curtains of fine twined linen were required for the covering of the Tabernacle.

One hundred cubits of linen, supported by *twenty* pillars, resting on *twenty* sockets of brass, were required for the south side of the Court; a similar number for the north side; for the breadth *fifty* cubits of hanging, supported by *ten* pillars, resting on *ten* sockets of brass.

Fifteen cubits of hanging were suspended on either side of the Gate of the Court, making *thirty* in all.

Twenty cubits of hanging of blue and scarlet and purple and fine twined linen, wrought with needlework, were needed with pillars *four* and sockets of brass *four*. This entrance set forth Christ as the only Way to God, and the *four* pillars and sockets set forth the universal aspect of the presentation of Christ, as the only Saviour for mankind.

Twenty gerahs, we are specifically informed, made up the half shekel of silver, demanded of all males from twenty years old and upward as "atonement money". This produced *one hundred talents, and a thousand seven hundred and three score and fifteen shekels of silver*, computed to weigh about four tons of silver. *One hundred* talents were used for the *one hundred* sockets of silver. The residue was used in the hooks and filleting of the *sixty* pillars of the Court, *twenty* on the south side, *twenty* on the north side, *ten* westward, *ten* eastward.

We content ourselves with giving these details, as they will be explained more fully later on. Suffice it to say that the number *five* and its multiples are employed in a striking way in the construction of the Tabernacle.

THE SIGNIFICANCE OF THE NUMBER SEVEN

SEVEN IS THE NUMBER DENOTING DIVINE PERFECTION.

Six is the number denoting the height of human attainment, which must ever come short of perfection.

THE SEVENTH DAY MARKED THE COMPLETION AND PERFECTION OF GOD'S CREATORIAL WORK.

"THE SEVEN SPIRITS WHICH ARE BEFORE HIS THRONE" (REVELATION 1:4)

denote the perfection of the activities of God, the Holy Spirit.

SEVEN WAS THE NUMBER OF THE BRANCHES OF THE GOLDEN CANDLESTICK.

SEVEN WAS THE NUMBER OF THE ITEMS THAT WENT TO FURNISH THE TABERNACLE:—

1. *The Ark.*
2. *The Mercy Seat.*
3. *The Shewbread Table.*
4. *The Golden Candlestick.*
5. *The Brazen Altar.*
6. *The Brazen Laver.*
7. *The Golden Altar of Incense.*

The first *five* set forth God coming *out to man*, making Himself known as a pardoning God on the ground of the atoning sacrifice of our Lord on the cross. The last *two* set forth the worshipper's going *in to God*, setting forth the work of Christ as our High Priest, as the first *five* set Him forth as the Apostle of our profession. It is in this order they are set forth in Scripture.

THE SIGNIFICANCE OF THE NUMBER TWELVE

TWELVE IS THE NUMBER THAT SETS FORTH ADMINISTRATION.

TWELVE IS THE NUMBER OF MONTHS IN THE YEAR,

setting forth God's administration in nature.

TWELVE IS THE NUMBER OF THE TRIBES OF ISRAEL,

setting forth God's administration in government on behalf of His earthly people.

The Encampment of Zebulun, Judah and Issachar
Moses, Aaron and his Sons

The Only Entrance — John 10:9

East Side

Door: 20 cubits

Entrance
John 14:6

Seeker
Matthew 7:7

Saved
Ephesians 2:8

Brazen Altar

5 cubits square
3 cubits high

Scale: 1 inch to 20 cubits

The Encampment of Asher, Dan and Naphtali

North Side: 100 cubits

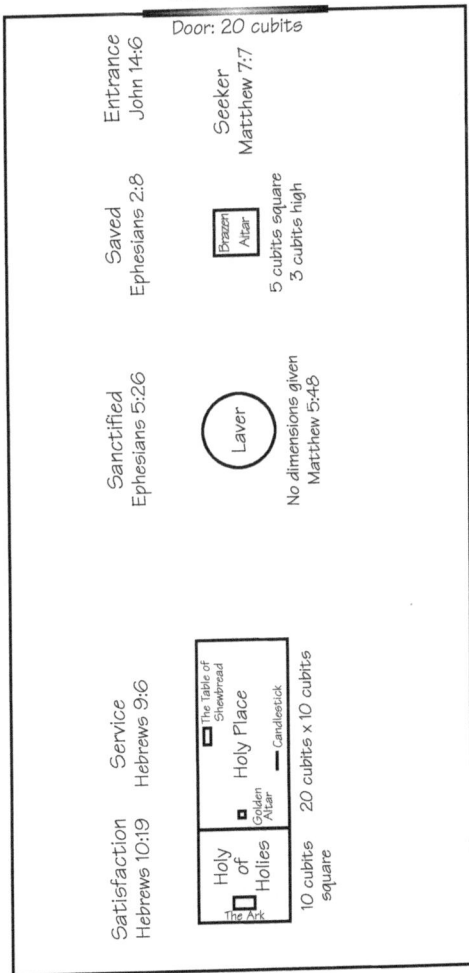

Sanctified
Ephesians 5:26

Laver

No dimensions given
Matthew 5:48

South Side: 100 cubits

The Encampment of Simeon, Reuben and Gad

Service
Hebrews 9:6

The Table of Shewbread

Holy Place

Candlestick

20 cubits x 10 cubits

Golden Altar

Satisfaction
Hebrews 10:19

Holy of Holies

The Ark

10 cubits square

West Side: 50 cubits

The Encampment of Benjamin, Ephraim and Manasseh

TWELVE WAS THE NUMBER OF LOAVES ON THE SHEWBREAD TABLE,

setting forth God's administration in the support and maintenance of His people.

TWELVE WAS THE NUMBER OF THE NAMES ENGRAVED ON THE SHOULDER PLATES OF THE HIGH PRIEST,

setting forth the Lord's administration in the support and maintenance of His people.

TWELVE WAS THE NUMBER OF PRECIOUS STONES IN THE BREAST-PLATE OF THE HIGH PRIEST,

setting forth our Lord's administration in love in the representation of His people in the presence of God. He appears "in the presence of God for us" (Hebrews 9:24).

TWELVE WAS THE NUMBER OF THE APOSTLES OF OUR LORD,

setting forth His administration in Christianity.

They were bidden to go into all the world and preach the Gospel to every creature. The Church is "built upon the foundation of the Apostles and Prophets, Jesus Christ Himself being the Chief Corner Stone" (Ephesians 2:20).

TWELVE IS A NUMBER THAT STRONGLY MARKS THE STRUCTURE OF THE HOLY CITY,

symbolizing the Church in administrative display in the Millennium (Revelation 21). It had

1. *Twelve Gates [, Angels and names]*.
2. *Twelve Foundations*.
3. *Twelve names in the Foundation*.
4. *Twelve kinds of precious stones in the Foundation*.
5. *Twelve Gates*.
6. *Twelve Pearls in the twelve Gates*.
7. *Twelve thousand furlongs was the breadth, and length and height of the City*.

8. *One hundred and forty-four cubits* (12 x 12) *was the measure of the Wall.*

9. *Twelve manner of fruits were borne on the Tree of Life in the Paradise of God during the twelve months of the year.*

THE SIGNIFICANCE OF THE NUMBER FORTY

FORTY IS COMPOUNDED OF TEN TIMES FOUR.

Ten is the full measure of man's responsibility Godward and manward, *four* representing that which is *universal.* It sets forth the full measure of probation and testing.

FORTY DAYS WAS THE PERIOD THAT THE FLOOD PREVAILED UPON THE EARTH,

a *universal* catastrophe.

FORTY DAYS WAS THE TIME THAT NOAH WAITED

after the waters of the Flood decreased before he opened the window of the Ark, and sent forth the raven, a waiting time before a new world order began.

FORTY YEARS OLD WAS MOSES WHEN HE FLED FROM EGYPT;

forty years later God commissioned him to become the deliverer of His people; *forty* years later he died.

FORTY YEARS MARKED THE LENGTH OF THE WILDERNESS JOURNEY OF THE CHILDREN OF ISRAEL,

the period of their testing.

FORTY YEARS MARKED THE LENGTH OF THE REIGNS OF SAUL, DAVID, AND SOLOMON,

a period of testing as how they would fulfil their responsibility towards God and man in the position of being Kings over God's earthly people.

FORTY DAYS WAS THE TIME GIVEN FOR NINEVEH TO REPENT,

and avert the destruction of their great city. God gives ample time for every person in the world to repent.

FORTY DAYS WAS THE LENGTH OF THE LORD'S TEMPTATION IN THE WILDERNESS,

Surely He was a *universal* Figure, and upon His triumph over Satan depended the blessing of the whole world.

FORTY DAYS WAS THE PERIOD BETWEEN THE LORD'S GLORIOUS RESURRECTION

and His ascension to Heaven, a long enough period to fully establish before many witnesses that He had indeed risen from the dead in the triumph of His finished work of atonement on the cross.

A good deal more might be said on this interesting subject, but space forbids.

NOTE

Some may reason that God would not stoop to mark His revelation with specific numbers, carrying a special meaning in their use. Astronomers and naturalists testify to the way God has stamped numbers upon His material creation. For instance, Indian corn is set in rows, which are always *even* and never *odd*. A farmer looked for twenty-seven years to find a "cob" with an *odd* number of rows without success. One other instance of numbers stamped on creation may suffice. The period of gestation with:-

The Mouse is	21	(3 x 7) days
The Hare and Rat	28	(4 x 7) days
The Cat	56	(8 x 7) days
The Dog	63	(9 x 7) days
The Lion	98	(14 x 7) days
The Sheep	147	(21 x 7) days
Human beings	280	(40 x 7) days

Note how all the periods are multiples of seven. Can we say this is a mere coincidence, or is it a design of God? Clearly the latter. God is the God of *nature*, and the God of *revelation*, and He has seen fit to stamp numbers on both.

In Daniel 8:13 we read: "Then I heard one saint speaking, and another saint said unto *that certain saint* which spake, How long shall be the vision concerning the daily sacrifice and the transgression of desolation, to give both the sanctuary and the host to be trodden under foot?" We quote this passage for the expression *"that certain saint"*. We are told by a competent authority this expression bears the significance of "a certain unknown person". In the margin of our Authorized Bible we read this person is described as *"the numberer of secrets, or the wonderful numberer"*, in the Hebrew the name "Palmoni", meaning a wonderful numberer, as the margin states. Does it not look as if there is appointed some angel, whose province is to deal with numbers?

Chapter 3:
Things Worthy of Note in Connection with the Tabernacle and its Service

A good deal of discussion has occurred over the meaning of the word, ATONEMENT; a word only to be found in the Old Testament, though the thought connected with the word is amply set forth in the New Testament. Indeed, it can be truly said that the word only occurs in the Old Testament, *but not the thing itself.* That could not be known in connection with Jewish sacrifices, which could never put away sin. Atonement itself is only found in the New Testament, for it is only known in the atoning sacrifice of the Son of God on Calvary's cross.

A great deal of unhappy modernistic capital has been made out of the meaning of the English word, AT-ONE-MENT, treating it as no more than two parties coming to an agreement. If the English word were the *exact* translation of the Hebrew word employed, then the meaning of the English word—ATONEMENT—would be significant. As a matter of fact, this not being the case, we must fix our attention on the meaning of the Hebrew word translated *atonement* in our Bible. The Hebrew word employed is

Kaphar, which means to cover. It is only by the death of Christ, by His atoning blood, that sin is covered, and its consequences averted. So we read, "Blessed is he whose transgression is forgiven, whose sin is covered [Hebrew, *Kasah*]" (Psalm 32:1). "Thou hast forgiven the iniquity of Thy people, Thou hast covered [Hebrew, *Kasah*] all their sin" (Psalm 85:2). *Kaphar* and *Kasah* both mean to cover. "It is the blood that maketh an atonement [Hebrew, *Kaphar*] for the soul" (Leviticus 17:11). How beautifully the New Testament answers to all this, "The blood of Jesus Christ His Son cleanseth us from all sin" (1 John 1:7).

Our first parents were *covered* by coats of skins, procured by the death of innocent victims, by blood-shedding, typical of redemption. Noah's Ark was *covered* by pitch within and without, so that it passed safely through the waters of judgment. The children of Israel were *covered* in their tents when Balaam looked upon them; and, bidden to curse, could only bless, typical of the result of the atoning sacrifice of Christ, when the believer is looked upon as blessed of God, which blessing is for ever his. God can be, and is, righteous in blessing the believing sinner. Let nothing weaken our conception of the grand atonement of our Lord Jesus Christ.

Wherever the word "brass" is used in Scripture it should be rendered *copper*, as already noted. Copper is a pure metal, and is fire-resisting in the highest degree among the metals.

The following table gives the degree of heat that the following metals will stand, beyond which they would melt:—

Brass	–	1650° Fahrenheit
Silver	–	1761° Fahrenheit

Gold	–	1946° Fahrenheit
Copper	–	1982° Fahrenheit

The word "Candlestick" (Exodus 25:31, [AV]) should be correctly translated Lampstand. The context shows this, for it was fed with oil. But, as already stated, we will adhere to the word employed in our Bible to save confusion.

It must be carefully noted that not only are there many types in connection with the Tabernacle, but there are also *contrasts*. This must be so seeing the Antitype is none less than the Son of God, and what type can adequately set Him forth in all His glorious fullness, or the wonderful results that flow from His death?

Let one instance here suffice. In the Tabernacle none but a priest could enter the Holy Place, and none but the High Priest could enter into the Holiest of All, and that but once a year.

In Christianity every believing sinner is a priest, and has liberty to enter the Holiest by the blood of Jesus at all times, that is to be consciously in God's presence. Not one person once a year, but *all* believers at *all* times. How great is the contrast!

> *"The veil is rent, our souls draw near*
> *Unto a throne of grace;*
> *The merits of the Lord appear,*
> *They fill the holy place."*

There was an ascending scale in connection with the Tabernacle. The metals used were:—

1.	In the Court	–	brass and silver
2.	In the Holy Place	–	silver and gold
3.	In the Holiest of All	–	pure gold alone

In the Court the ordinary person could come.

In the Holy Place the priests only.

In the Holiest of All the High Priest alone.

WHAT THERE WAS NOT IN THE TABERNACLE

We can learn a good deal from the silence as well as the speech of Scripture, by its omissions as well as by what it states.

As we enter the Tabernacle we notice there is *no* lock or bolt on the entrance. God would signify that He is ready at all times for the approach of the sinner.

THERE WERE NO CHERUBIMS, SYMBOLIZING JUDGMENT,

worked in the Gate of the Court, nor on the Door of the Tent, whilst cherubims were worked on the Vail separating the Holy Place from the Holiest of All.

God would thus signify His perfect grace in meeting the needy sinner.

THERE WERE NO STEPS TO THE ALTAR.

"Neither shalt thou go up by steps unto mine Altar, that thy nakedness be not discovered thereon" (Exodus 20:26). God would thus teach us that no preparation on our side will help us to come into His presence, that turning over a new leaf, dropping sinful habits, becoming religious, doing the best we can, is not the way of approach. The sacrificial death of Christ *alone* and *fully* suffices. "By grace are ye saved, through faith; and that not of yourselves: it is the gift of God: not of works, lest any man should boast" (Ephesians 2:8-9). *No* steps to the Altar.

THERE WAS NO MEASUREMENT FOR THE BRAZEN LAVER.

The Laver filled with water, typical of the cleansing quality of the word of God, sets forth the holiness that befits those who have to do with God, and there is no limit to that. "Be ye therefore perfect, even as your Father which is in Heaven is perfect" (Matthew 5:48).

THERE WAS NO EXTINGUISHER PROVIDED FOR THE GOLDEN CANDLESTICK.

God would ever give to His people the light they need. Christ is our light. We are the children of light. There is no withdrawal of that at any time.

THERE WAS NO WINDOW PROVIDED FOR THE TABERNACLE.

No light of nature was needed where God Himself provided the light. What a lesson for the believer to learn! All the fullness of the Godhead resides in a blessed Man risen and exalted, even in our Lord Jesus Christ. We are complete in Him, and need no light of nature. We have all spiritual knowledge communicated to us in the Holy Scriptures, and we have an infallible Teacher, the Holy Spirit of God.

THERE WAS NO SEAT PROVIDED FOR THE PRIESTS,

for their work was ineffectual, only shadows and types, wonderful as they were, so we read, "Every priest *standeth* daily ministering and offering oftentimes the same sacrifices, which can never take away sins: but this man [*the Lord Jesus Christ*], after He had offered one sacrifice for sins for ever, *sat down* on the right hand of God" (Hebrews 10:11-12). Thus we have the contrast we spoke of, in this case between the *incomplete* work of the priests, and the *completed* work of Christ.

The following measurement and weights may be useful to the reader [3]:—

1 cubit	1 foot, 9.888 inches
1 shekel (silver)	2s. 3.37d. (at 5s. an ounce)

1 talent of silver	£342 3s. 9d.
1 talent of gold	£5,475

We must remember the purchasing power of money has fluctuated greatly at various times; in olden times it was far greater than at the present time.

THERE WERE TWO ARKS

Deuteronomy 10:1-5 relates how the Lord instructed Moses to make an Ark of shittim wood, and bring it with two Tables of stone up to the Holy Mount, when he went the second time into God's presence, just after the terrible incident of the idolatry of the Golden Calf. So Moses made an Ark of shittim wood, and placed the two Tables of stone in it, thus showing that the law pure and simple was never brought into the midst of Israel, but that God had Christ, and the way of blessing in sovereign grace in the atoning death of Christ ever before Him, even for the sinner, who had broken the law.

When God called Moses the first time up to the Holy Mount with all its accompanying signs and sounds, the whole Mount shaking, the thunders and lightnings, the thick cloud covering the Mount, the trumpet loud sounding and waxing louder and louder, we are told that Moses said, "I exceedingly fear and quake" (Hebrews 12:21). And what was the first commandment of the ten? We read, "Thou shalt have no other gods before Me. Thou shalt not make unto thee any graven image, or any likeness of any thing that is in heaven above, or that is in the earth beneath, or that is in the water under the earth: thou shalt not bow down thyself to them, nor serve them: for I the LORD thy God am a jealous God, visiting the iniquity of the fathers upon the children unto the third and fourth generation of them that hate Me" (Exodus 20:3-5).

As Moses came down the Mount with the two naked Tables of stone in his hands, he heard the voice of singing. When he got within sight of the camp, it was to see the golden calf, and the people stripped naked, according to the horrible idolatrous custom of heathen lands, dancing before it.

The very first commandment was thus most grievously broken. The anger of Moses waxed hot, and he cast the Tables out of his hands, and brake them beneath the Mount. What an ordeal for Moses! He could well realize that to bring the naked Tables of the law into the camp would have meant the destruction of the whole camp, for all were involved from Aaron downwards in this terrible idolatry.

What was he to do? He would have to think rapidly and decisively. The Tables of stone had been furnished by God Himself, and the Ten Commandments were written by His own fingers. It was a tremendous thing to smash them on the mountain side. It showed the spiritual intuition and great moral courage of this wonderful servant of God.

So now we see the provision of God in calling Moses to bring an Ark of shittim wood in order that the naked law might not be carried into the camp. The two Tables, the Tables of the Testimony, were put inside the Ark, prefiguring that there would come One, who would perfectly keep the law, hide it in His heart, and that God would have One upon whom He could call to effect blessing for those who broke the law and were repentant.

Not only were the Ten Commandments communicated to Moses, but at the same time all the instructions as to the Tabernacle and the Sacrifices were given. This shows that the law pure and simple was never given to man, but that with it the way was pointed out by shadows, types and prophecies, how sinful men could approach God through the atoning sacrifice of our Lord.

The Ark of shittim wood that Moses made was only temporary, for we read in Exodus 37 how the wise-hearted Bezaleel made an Ark of shittim wood, covering it with "pure gold", and in this Ark the Tables of Testimony were eventually placed. The interval between Moses receiving the law, and the setting up of the Tabernacle was thus mercifully bridged.

THE EASTWARD POSITION

The Tabernacle was always pitched towards the east, so that the Mercy Seat should face in that direction. The Gate of the Court (Exodus 27:13-14) was *eastwards*. The blood of the Sin offering was sprinkled on the Mercy Seat *eastward* (Leviticus 16:14). What was the reason for this? As the sun arises in the east, so the Tabernacle was pitched in that direction, typical of the time when "The Sun of righteousness [*even our Lord Jesus Christ*] shall arise with healing in His wings" (Malachi 4:2), bringing peace and security, and God's *"new order"* to this troubled world. We read, "The children of Israel set forward ... and they journeyed ... *toward the sunrising"* (Numbers 21:10-11). "The path of the just is as the shining light that shineth more and more unto the perfect day" (Proverbs 4:18).

The ritualist, who affects the eastward position, only proclaims by his slavish and unscriptural adherence to the "shadow", that he knows little or nothing of the glorious Substance, the Fulfiller of these types, our Lord and Saviour. Ritualism, moral deadness, spiritual darkness, superstition, bigotry, and persecution of what is true and real, often go together. It is to be feared that the Eastward Position, as practised by the ritualist, is one of the means by which an arrogant priesthood seeks to enslave the laity.

DIVINE GUIDANCE

"The LORD your God ... went in the way before you, to search you out a place to pitch your tents in, in fire by night, to show you by what way ye should go, and in a cloud by day" (Deuteronomy 1:32-33). When Moses completed the rearing of the Tabernacle, a cloud covered the Tent of the Congregation, and the glory of the Lord filled the Tabernacle. Provision was thus made for Divine guidance for the people in their journey. When the cloud was stationary the people rested; when it moved, they moved and followed the direction it took. If the journey were by night, the fire was their sufficient guide. "He spread a cloud for a covering; and fire to give light in the night" (Psalm 105:39).

Thus God would teach us the lesson of dependence, and how we should ever seek His guidance. We are not sufficient of ourselves to map out our own paths, whether as individuals, or in relation to the Church of God. How full of thoughtful care are all God's ways. We may well trust Him to do far better for us than we can do for ourselves.

Chapter 4:
The Ark, Mercy Seat, and Cherubims

READ EXODUS 25:10-22; LEVITICUS 16:14; HEBREWS 9:1-5; ROMANS 3:24-26

A few general remarks may profitably take their place here. The Divine Architect of the Tabernacle did not follow the way of ordinary custom. If an architect were asked to prepare a royal palace for the reception of a royal throne, he would naturally begin with the foundation, proceed with the walls, and finally put on the roof. Then when the building was finished, the furniture would be installed, the noblest setting of which would be the royal throne.

It is all the other way in relation to the Tabernacle. The Ark with the Mercy Seat was *God's* throne, and this is the very first to be mentioned. The Ark and Mercy Seat set forth Christ in His Deity, Manhood, and atoning sacrifice on the cross of Calvary. Yet what can we say of our blessed Lord? He is at once the Foundation and the Topstone, and the Chief Corner Stone, the Alpha and the Omega, the Beginning and the Ending, the First and the Last. All truth circles round His Person and work, He is the great Mediator between God and men.

How truly John Newton, the erstwhile blasphemer, wrote:

> *"What think ye of Christ? is the test*
> *To try both your state and your scheme,*
> *You cannot be right in the rest,*
> *Unless you think rightly of Him."*

In enumerating the articles in the Tabernacle we find the Ark, Mercy Seat and Cherubims in the Holiest of All are first mentioned, then comes the Shewbread Table, and Golden Candlestick in the Holy Place. Though the beautiful Golden Altar of Incense was also in the Holy Place, nothing is said about it till Exodus 30 is reached. Proceeding outside we find the Brazen Altar and the Court of the Tabernacle are mentioned, but nothing, till Exodus 30 is reached, is said of the Brazen Laver, though it stood in the Court. Why should the Golden Altar, and the Laver be thus omitted? We have heard of infidels pointing triumphantly at this *apparent* omission, and asking: How can you call the Bible inspired when there are such careless and obvious blunders?

On the contrary this order is just what stamps the Bible as inspired. To make our meaning plain we would draw attention to the Scripture, "Wherefore, holy brethren, partakers of the heavenly calling, consider the Apostle and High Priest of our profession, Christ Jesus" (Hebrews 3:1). Our Lord is both Apostle and High Priest. What is the difference between the offices of Apostle and High Priest?

The Apostle brings *God* TO MAN for his eternal blessing.

The High Priest brings *men* TO GOD for worship.

The Ark, Mercy Seat, Shewbread Table, Candlestick, and Brazen Altar all typify Christ as the Apostle, the sent One of the Father, the great Mediator between God and man, and most especially in His atoning death, the only means by which blessing can come to sinful man.

The Golden Altar and Brazen Laver on the other hand set forth Christ, as the High Priest of our profession, supporting His people in the presence of God. The Brazen Laver, filled with water, was where the priests *going in* to the service of the Sanctuary washed their feet and hands to ensure cleanliness as they went into God's presence. The Golden Altar set forth the happy service of the priest as a worshipper offering incense, symbolical of presenting Christ in all the sweet savour of His sacrifice to God.

Exodus 25, to the end of chapter 27, gives us the instructions as to the articles in the Tabernacle that present symbolically Christ as the Apostle of our profession, God coming out to man in Christ, full of grace and mercy.

Exodus 28 tells us of the garments of glory and beauty of the High Priest, and of the garments of the priests.

Exodus 29 gives us the consecration of the High Priest and priests. Not till we have the High Priest and priests consecrated could there be the setting forth of Christ, as the High Priest of our profession. So Exodus 30 tells us of the Golden Altar of Incense, and the Brazen Laver, both speaking of man *going in* as a worshipper into God's holy presence.

So we see how inspired is the narration of Scripture. How foolish to impose the littleness of human thought of what should be, or should not be, instead of humbly seeking the thoughts of the Divine mind. "As the heavens are higher than the earth, so are ... My thoughts than your thoughts" (Isaiah 55:9), God says.

Another instance of Divine order is seen in Exodus 26. Human architects would scoff at a builder, seeking to arrange the roof before the walls were erected. Yet this is the order followed out in this chapter. The four curtains, or coverings, of the Tabernacle are detailed for us before the boards of the Tabernacle are spoken of. In the last great war the word "cover" was much in vogue. To help the infantry and artillerymen to carry on their land operations, it was found necessary to afford "air cover". Here the curtains formed the covering of the Tabernacle, typical of Christ in His various official glories, whilst the boards speak of believers being builded together to be a habitation of God by the Spirit. How right it is that Christ should be seen as the cover, before the walls, typical of believers, were erected, for it is in virtue of who He is, and what He has done, that believers get their place before Him.

THE ARK

The Ark was made of shittim wood, two-and-a-half cubits long, by a cubit-and-a-half wide, and a cubit-and-a-half high. It was covered with pure gold inside and out, and a crown, or ledge of gold, placed around it. Here we have typified very beautifully the Deity and Manhood of our Lord Jesus Christ. The shittim wood, the acacia wood of the desert, set forth the Humanity of our blessed Lord; the pure gold, His Deity. The crown, or ledge of gold round about, taught how God jealously guards these great truths of the Deity and Manhood of our Lord.

"No man knoweth the Son but the Father" (Matthew 11:27) is a wonderful statement, settling once and for ever the thus-far-and-no-further of our knowledge in this direction. Nearly all the great heresies that have rent the Church of God from the time of Arius downward have originated in faulty and speculative theories as to the truth of Christ's Person. Our only sure course is to adhere to the very words of Scripture, and to refuse speculation into mysteries unrevealed. Only the Father knows the Son; therefore the manner in which Deity and Manhood are united in Him is beyond our scrutiny.

"Thou art the Christ, the Son of the living God" (Matthew 16:16) was the confession of the Apostle Peter. Our Lord traced his knowledge to the fact that it had been revealed to him by the Father, and affirmed that upon the truth of Christ's Person the Church of God should be built, and the gates of Hades should not prevail against it. Although Peter knew the Lord, as all believers do, yet neither he nor they shall ever fathom the inscrutable depths of His Person.

The poet [Frederick William Faber] sang truly and wisely:

"'Tis darkness to my intellect,
But sunshine to my heart."

How God, the Son, could become Man, and yet in becoming Man, never cease to be God, and yet be one undivided Person, is surely past the creature's comprehension, but it is the truth as presented in Scripture. We have the clear statements:—

"The Word was God" (John 1:1).

"The Word was made flesh" (John 1:14).

It is amazing to contemplate that the One, who wearied with His journey, and who sat on Sychar's well; the One, whose feet were washed by the tears of a penitent woman; and above all the One, who died for us on the cross of Calvary, was none the less than "The Mighty God, The Everlasting Father, The Prince of Peace" (Isaiah 9:6). "He was crucified through weakness" (2 Corinthians 13:4), yet at that very moment was "upholding all things by the word of His power" (Hebrews 1:3). We may not understand how this can be, but we can humbly adore Him, who is "Emmanuel, which, being interpreted, is GOD with us" (Matthew 1:23).

Right through Scripture the Godhead of Jesus is maintained. He is the Eternal Son in the Unity of the Godhead—Father, Son and Holy Spirit, One God, blessed for ever. He claimed equality with the Father. He received unquestioned the worship of His disciples. His omnipotence proclaimed His Godhead.

When the frightened disciples awoke their Master as He lay asleep in the hinder part of the ship as it tossed in the storm on the lake, and cried, "Master, Master, we perish", He arose, and rebuked the wind and the raging of the sea, and there was a great calm. Astounded beyond measure, the disciples exclaimed, "What manner of man is this! for He commandeth even the winds and water, and they obey

Him" (Luke 8:25), as much as to say that this was power above that of man, and they were right.

His power, even to the raising of the dead, proclaimed His Godhead. But it may be said, Did not the Apostle Peter raise up Dorcas to life again? The answer is that the Lord's servants did not raise the dead by their own power but *in the name of the Lord*, whereas the Lord raised the dead by His OWN word of power. He invoked no name as His disciples did. He said to the young man of Nain, as he was being carried to his funeral, "Young man, I say unto thee, Arise" (Luke 7:14). Our Lord was "God ... manifest in the flesh" (1 Timothy 3:16). He became a true Man, blessed be His name, and atoned for sin at the cross of Calvary. God and Man—one Christ, one glorious Person—is presented to our faith and for our homage.

RINGS AND STAVES

There were four rings of gold, one in each corner of the Ark. Through these, staves of shittim wood covered with gold were placed, thus providing for the transport of the Ark from place to place. The staves were not to be withdrawn till the Ark found its final resting place in the Temple in the land. Thus God would teach us that we are still in the wilderness.

Only the priests were allowed to carry the Ark, thus showing that only true believers have right thoughts of Christ. Alas! man makes his new cart of human theology, and the Uzzahs of Higher Criticism seek to steady that which, apparently to them, but not in reality, threatens to fall, only to their own destruction.

When one of these modern Uzzahs of unitarian taint was presenting Christ as the great Model and Example for mankind, a woman's shrill voice was heard from the outskirts of the crowd, saying, "I say, Mister, your rope is not long enough to reach a sinner like me." How true is the remark, "When all the Higher Critics have had their say, and all the shouting has ceased, the sixty-six books of the Bible will rise up, and cry in unison, 'Sirs, do yourselves no harm, for we are all here'."

Right thoughts of Christ are vital to Christianity. Let us be crystal clear as to this. We cannot afford to make a mistake. "He that believeth on Him is not condemned: but he that believeth not is condemned already, because he hath not believed in the name of the only begotten Son of God" (John 3:18).

THE TESTIMONY

The Testimony, that is the two Tables of Stone on which the ten commandments were written by the finger of God, was placed in the Ark, which Moses was commanded to make. This symbolized how perfectly our Lord would keep the law. "Lo, I come (in the volume of the book it is written of Me) to do Thy will, O God" (Hebrews 10:7).

Some hold the erroneous idea that Christ's perfect keeping of the law atoned for their lack of doing so. They hold that credit is thereby put to their account, and thus they are accounted righteous. It is, indeed, true, that if our Lord had not kept the law perfectly, He could not have been our Saviour, but it needed a sinless Sacrifice upon whom death had no claim to take the sinner's place and room. That this is necessary, that it is our Lord's atoning death, and not His spotless life that is sufficient, is shown by the words, "Without shedding of blood is no remission" (Hebrews 9:22). "As Moses lifted up the serpent in the wilderness, even so MUST the Son of Man be lifted up" (John 3:14).

The expression, "The Ark of the Testimony", has been sadly perverted by some to mean exclusively the testimony of a body of believers, who profess to be faithful to the truth amid general unfaithfulness. Such will use the ignorant and arrogant expression, "The Ark of the Testimony is with Us." The Ark of the Testimony typifies Christ, and no body of believers can appropriate Him as their exclusive possession, any more than any country can claim the sun as their exclusive possession, as it marches across the sky. The worst form of heresy in the early Church was seen in some saying, "I [*am*] of Christ" (1 Corinthians 1:12), claiming Christ for a party, and His name and presence in their midst as a distinguishing feature in contradistinction to other Christians.

THE MERCY SEAT

The Mercy Seat consisted of a slab of pure gold, stained with the blood of the Sin Offering on the Great Day of Atonement, which rested above upon the Ark. Only on that day, and by the High Priest alone, could entrance be made into the Holiest of All in order to sprinkle the blood once upon the Mercy Seat eastward, and seven times before it. The *gold* typified Divine righteousness. Without Divine righteousness being satisfied there could not be any flowing out of God's grace to guilty man. The blood of the Sin Offering typified the precious blood of Christ. As it were, the *gold* demanded righteous satisfaction, the blood met that demand, and so it became a Mercy Seat.

Have we the thought of the Mercy Seat in the New Testament? Yes, for we read, "And over it the cherubims of glory shadowing the Mercy Seat [Greek, *hilasterion*]" (Hebrews 9:5). "Whom [*Christ*] God hath set forth to be a propitiation [Greek, *hilasterion*] through faith in His blood" (Romans 3:25). "He is the propitiation [Greek, *hilasmos*] for our sins" (1 John 2:2). "God ... sent His Son to be the propitiation [Greek, *hilasmos*] for our sins" (1 John 4:10). Thus the New Testament shows clearly that Mercy Seat and propitiation is one and the same word. Thus the Old and New Testament clasp hands.

THE CHERUBIMS

Cherubims, angelic creatures, were God's messengers of judgment. Cherubims and a flaming sword barred our fallen and sinful first parents' access to the Tree of Life, lest they should eat of it, and live for ever. They stood as representative of God's righteous judgment: "Justice and judgment are the habitation of Thy throne" (Psalm 89:14).

Two cherubims of gold, beaten of one piece (see Exodus 37:7) with outstretched wings covering the Mercy Seat, their faces looking towards each other, and downward towards the Mercy Seat, were placed on the top of the Mercy Seat, as it rested on the Ark.

Their outstretched wings symbolized the *instant* readiness to execute judgment, nay, the absolute necessity for God's righteousness to be upheld when His laws are violated. The camp of Israel contained sinners enough to call forth the full activity, which they symbolized. Yet there they stood, gazing on the golden blood-stained Mercy Seat, surely indicating that God's claims had been fully met, and that justice was satisfied.

Of course we must remember that the types in themselves never met God's claims, but what they typified did. We must look past the types to the great Antitype, and there see in Christ and His atoning work the answer, and only answer, to it all. How it sets forth the meaning of "Mercy and truth are met together; righteousness and peace have kissed each other" (Psalm 85:10).

THREE THINGS IN THE ARK

Hebrews 9:4 tells us there were three things in the Ark—
"the Golden Pot that had manna, and Aaron's rod that
budded, and the Tables of the Covenant".

THE GOLDEN POT THAT HAD MANNA

The golden pot that had manna was a memorial of God's
sustainment of His people in the wilderness. For forty
years this great people were supported in a place where
earthly sustenance was absent. God was enough. Morning
by morning the manna fell. "Angels' food" it was called.
In appearance it was small and round, like hoar frost upon
the ground. In colour it was white and it tasted like honey.

Manna is a pure Hebrew word, meaning, What is it? The
children of Israel could not give it a name. It fell miracu-
lously from heaven, and was outside the range of human
experience as to its origin.

The manna was *small*, typical of Christ, whose earthly circumstances were humble and lowly. He came not with
pomp of monarch, nor with triumph of conqueror, but in
lowly guise. He was born in a stable, and cradled in a
manger. It could be said of Him, "The foxes have holes
and the birds of the air have nests; but the Son of Man
hath not where to lay His head" (Matthew 8:20). His
deathbed was a cross of shame. He lay in a borrowed
grave. Was there ever such an appeal as this?

The manna was *round*, typical of the accessibility of
Christ. A round thing—unlike a square, or an oblong, or
oval—is equally near the centre wherever you may touch
the circumference. *Round* would set forth how accessible
our Lord was to young and old, rich and poor, religious
and irreligious. The woman that was a sinner; Mary
Magdalene, out of whom was cast seven devils; the dying

thief; the children whom the disciples would have driven away—all alike could reach Him and be blessed.

Manna was like coriander seed and *white* in colour, typical of the pure and lovely life of our Lord. Its taste was like wafer made with honey, typical of the sweetness found in Him. "I sat down under His shadow with great delight, and His fruit was sweet to my taste" (Song of Solomon 2:3).

It had to be gathered in the morning, illustrating that there must needs be Divine energy for the appropriation of Christ. Further, what was gathered had to be eaten the day it was gathered. Kept over till the morning, it would breed worms and stink, thus teaching a salutary lesson that there must be *present* communion.

There was, however, a provision made, that on the sixth day of the week, they should gather a double portion, so as to provide for the needs of the Sabbath when they were not allowed to work.

Those, who attempt to "traffic in unfelt truth", relying on mere memory and knowledge, treating Divine things in a merely intellectual way, will find it only leads to corruption.

God would ever have in remembrance the Golden Pot that had manna as the memorial of how He met the needs of His people in the wilderness. God would never have us forget His grace and provision in the wilderness, not even in the glory.

AARON'S ROD THAT BUDDED

Aaron's rod that budded had a truly remarkable significance. Korah, a Levite, Dathan and Abiram, Reubenites, rebelled against Moses, in reality against God. They accused Moses and Aaron of taking too much upon themselves in appropriating religious service to the priesthood alone. They contended that all alike were competent to take part in this. It was an attack of religious democracy, and betokened no sense of the holiness of God's house, or of God's right to order things therein. The competence of man in the things of God was their claim, and their *blasphemy*.

If the reader will peruse Numbers 16 and 17, he will get the interesting and instructive details of this incident. Suffice it to say for our present purpose that when the test was made, and God had brought dire judgment on the rebels, He ordained a further test to show what His mind was as to the priesthood. Twelve rods were to be chosen, and each marked with the name of a tribe, Aaron's name to be written on the rod of Levi.

These rods were simply dry sticks. Put a live slip into the earth, and the ground will nurture the life in the slip, and it will take root, grow and bear fruit. Put a dry stick in the earth, and the ground can only rot the stick. The live slip will be "life unto life"; the dead stick "death unto death".

These dead rods were to be laid up before the Lord in the Tabernacle of Witness, and lo! in the morning a miracle had happened. Eleven sticks were dry sticks still, but Aaron's stick, dry like the others, had overnight burst into buds, bloomed blossoms, and yielded almonds.

The miracle was amazing. What did it signify? *It was clearly* LIFE *out of* DEATH. In this way God indicated that the priesthood should belong exclusively to Aaron and his sons. In this we learn a wonderful and fundamental lesson, that

CHRISTIANITY IS FOUNDED ON RESURRECTION.

Christ's resurrection is the witness of the triumph of His death, of God's full acceptance of the finished atoning work wrought out on Cavalry's cross.

There is a wonderful painting [by Sir Joseph Noel Paton] entitled, *Mors janua vitae, death* THE GATE *of life*; and this is just what Christianity is. But it is Christ's death, His triumphant death, which meeting all the claims of God's throne, has opened a new world, that resurrection scene of life and joy and worship, to the believer.

The priesthood of Christ is founded on His death and resurrection. His priesthood sustains His wilderness people till the heavenly Canaan is reached in association with Christ, the High Priest of our profession. But remember *all* believers in Christianity are priests. Wonderful privilege, but how little taken up!

THE TABLES OF THE COVENANT

When the Ark was put into its place in Solomon's Temple, we read, "There was nothing in the Ark save the two Tables which Moses put therein at Horeb, when the Lord made a covenant with the children of Israel, when they came out of Egypt" (2 Chronicles 5:10). The writer of the Hebrews enumerates three things, the golden pot of manna, Aaron's rod that budded, and the Tables of the Covenant, evidently referring to a different time.

The Tables of the Covenant placed in the Ark typified our Lord keeping the law in thought, word and deed. He "did no sin" (1 Peter 2:22); "In Him is no sin" (1 John 3:5); He "knew no sin" (2 Corinthians 5:21), is the threefold testimony of the Apostles Peter, John and Paul.

Chapter 5:
The Table of Shewbread

READ EXODUS 25:23-30; LEVITICUS 24:5-9

We pass from the Holiest of All, where were the Ark and Mercy Seat, and we enter the Holy Place. There we see the Table of Shewbread and the Golden Candlestick. The former is mentioned first. It was made of shittim wood covered with pure gold. Christ in His Godhead glory (pure gold), and in His Manhood (shittim wood), are here set forth.

This is the first time in Scripture the word Table [Hebrew, *shulchan*] is mentioned. The primary thought of a table is food and sustenance. So the Shewbread Table sets forth Christ as the Food of His people, not indeed here as in wilderness circumstances, that the manna met, but in Sanctuary service. It was the food of the priests.

The manna is the food we need in connection with wilderness circumstances, and there we are fed and nourished by the Lord's care of us in our trials, weaknesses, infirmities, bereavements, etc. All of us can tell the story of how we have been maintained in this way. But when we get into the assembly, or in private meditation, we find ourselves in association with a risen Christ, "accepted in the Beloved" (Ephesians 1:6), "blessed ... with all spiritual blessings in heavenly places in Christ" (Ephesians 1:3). We know the Father's love as revealed in and by His beloved Son, our Lord Jesus Christ. In such exercises we are in a region where there are no trials, no disappointments. We taste the heavenly side of things, and this is set forth in the type of The Shewbread Table.

THE MEASUREMENT OF THE TABLE OF SHEWBREAD

Whilst the length and breadth of the Table of Shewbread was less than that of the Ark, its height was the same. The lesser length and breadth would indicate that whilst the Ark and Mercy Seat have in view typically the whole world, the Table of Shewbread stands typically in relation to the Lord's people only. The Mercy Seat is available for all; the Shewbread Table was only for the priests. Their height being equal sets forth that the believer's communion is commensurate with the fullness of the place won through the atoning death of Christ.

TWO GOLDEN CROWNS

A crown of gold round about, and a border of a handsbreadth round about, and a golden crown for the border, spoke in a twofold way: (1) How God would jealously guard the truth of the Person of His beloved Son, and (2) How God would preserve His people in relation to Christ. This latter will be understood when we speak of the loaves as placed upon the Table.

RINGS, STAVES, AND VESSELS

The rings and staves emphasize, as in the case of the Ark, that we are in the wilderness, and not yet at home in the heavenly Canaan.

The dishes, spoons, covers and bowls, all made of pure gold signify typically that Divine things, God's sacred things, cannot be handled by the mind of man, they must be spiritually reached, appropriated and enjoyed. It is the Spirit of God alone, who can help us in this.

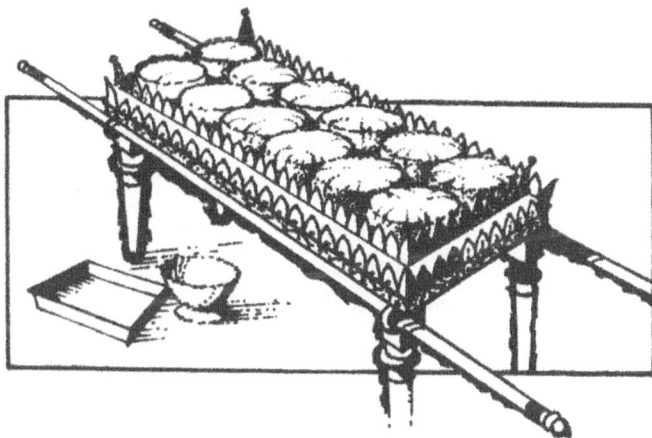

THE TWELVE LOAVES

Upon the Table were placed twelve cakes, or loaves. These represented the twelve tribes of Israel. It is true that only the priests could eat of the loaves, and that in the Holy Place, but they did so *representatively* for the whole of Israel. The priests were a tithe of all the children of Israel, and thus stood in a representative relation to the whole. This was all typical of the believer's portion. All believers are priests. Christ is the Food of *all* God's people. Alas! how little we appreciate this wealth of heavenly sustenance. We are often content to live in spiritual indigence, when we might live in spiritual affluence.

The cakes, or loaves, were to be made of fine flour, indicating the same truth as set forth in the fine linen, viz. [4], the spotless life of our Lord Jesus. Fine flour has no grit in it. Run your hand through flour, how smooth it is. With all of us how much grit and unevenness there is in our lives. With Him all was perfection.

In the case of our Lord He was distinguished from all others, because in Him was the blending of every grace and true quality in all their fullness and perfection. We cannot affirm He was one thing more than another. Where one is marked by failure in this, and failure in that, the Lord is marked off from us all, in that every true quality was fully matured and blended in Him.

The cakes, or loaves, were baked. Flour needs to be kneaded and baked in the oven before it is fit for food. This illustrates that Christ could not become the Food of His people save through death. It is His atoning death that enables the believer to feed on Him as the Food of His people.

Two tenth deals were in each loaf. The *tenth* speaks of responsibility being fully met. The *two* tenths speak of adequate testimony as to this.

These twelve loaves were set in two rows, six in each row, and frankincense put upon them, typical of how fragrant Christ is to God. Every Sabbath they were set in order before the Lord continually. They were for the food of Aaron and his sons in the Holy Place.

Chapter 6:
The Golden Candlestick

READ EXODUS 25:31-40; 27:20-21; LEVITICUS 24:1-4;
NUMBERS 8:1-4

The Golden Candlestick was properly a Lampstand, for it was fed with oil. In speaking of the Candlestick we must bear this in mind.

It was made of pure gold. Unlike the previous articles we have considered, no shittim wood entered into its construction, and no measurement is given as to its size. It weighed a talent of pure gold (114 lbs.), and was worth about £5,745 at the low valuation of those days [5]. It was beaten out of one piece, exquisitely proportioned and ornamented.

Just as the Table of Shewbread sets forth Christ as the *Food* of His people, so the Candlestick sets forth God's provision for the *Light* of His people.

There was no window in the Tabernacle. No light of nature entered the Holy Place. The light of the Golden Candlestick, and that alone, constituted the light of the Holy Place. It reminds us of the Scripture, "The city had no need of the sun, neither of the moon, to shine in it: for the glory of God did lighten it, and the Lamb is the light thereof" (Revelation 21:23).

Most evidently the Golden Candlestick is typical of our Lord. First it was made of "pure gold", always typical of our Lord's Godhead glory. Then it had no measurement, for it sets forth Christ *in glory* in all the fullness and blessedness of His person and work. We read, "Three bowls made like unto almonds with a knop [*bud*] and a flower in one branch; and three bowls made like almonds in the other branch, with a knop and a flower: so in the six branches that come out of the Candlestick. And in the Candlestick shall be four bowls made like unto almonds, with their knops and their flowers" (Exodus 25:33-34). We bring to mind what we said about Aaron's Rod that budded, blossomed and bore almonds overnight as typifying our Lord in His resurrection, which signified life out of death. These ornamentations link up with this teaching, and clearly show it is typical of Christ *in the place He has secured for us in resurrection* as the result of His atoning death. It is beautiful how Scriptures link up with each other, and confirm and make plain their meaning as they throw light upon each other.

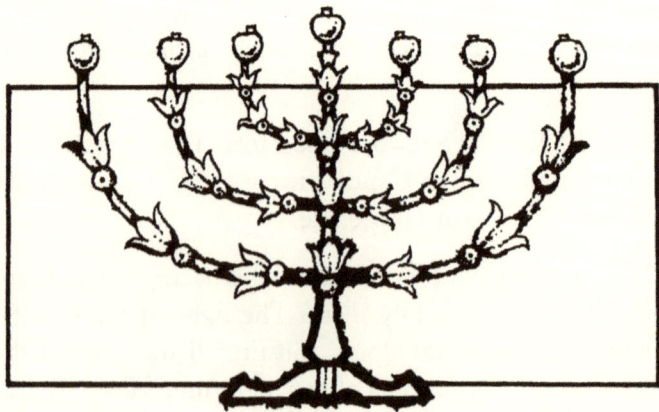

Thus far we have spoken of the Golden Candlestick as the *Light* BEARER. But what of the light itself? We know that these lamps were fed by oil, and oil is a figure of the third Person of the blessed Trinity, the Holy Spirit of God. How does the light shine for the Christian to-day? Christ is no longer on earth. He has ascended to the right hand of the Majesty on high. How, then, does the light shine to-day for the Christian? In answer we point out that our ascended Lord has sent the Holy Spirit into this world in a very special way in connection with the Church of God upon this earth. So we read, "When the Comforter is come, whom I will send unto you from the Father, even the Spirit of truth, which proceedeth from the Father, HE *shall testify of Me*" (John 15:26). We believe the oil is clearly typical of the Holy Spirit of God, who testifies of Christ, and this sheds the light of Christ into the hearts of believers.

Numbers 8:2 confirms this very beautifully. We read, "Speak unto Aaron, and say unto him, When thou lightest the lamps, the seven lamps shall give light *over against the Candlestick.*" Evidently the lamps were so arranged as to light up the beautiful Golden Candlestick, and its ornamentations of buds, blossoms, and almonds, setting forth the grand truth of life out of death, and that all our knowledge of, and blessing in Christ are founded on that glorious resurrection, which is proof of the acceptance of His atoning death by God, thus setting Him free to bless us in this wonderful way.

On each lateral stem of the Candlestick were three bowls, almond shape, with their knops (buds) and flowers. *Three* surely sets forth the full testimony of the Holy Spirit to the glory of Christ in His Person and work. The central stem had *four* bowls with knops and flowers, indicating that our Lord's Person and work, and the glory of them, is for the whole world. Alas! the whole world does not respond.

The Candlestick had seven stems, setting forth the many-sided activities of the Holy Spirit in His testimony to Christ. Four times over in the Book of Revelation does it speak of the *seven* Spirits of God. One passage in particular says, "There were *seven* lamps of fire burning before the throne, which are the *seven* Spirits of God" (Revelation 4:5). In Ephesians 4:4 we are told explicitly, "There is ... ONE Spirit." That is surely true. Though there were seven branches in the Candlestick, there was only ONE Candlestick. Seven lamps burning, yet only one pervading light.

Isaiah 11:1-2 may illustrate this. We read, "And there shall come forth a Rod out of the stem of Jesse, and a Branch shall grow out of His roots: and the Spirit of the LORD shall rest upon Him, the spirit of wisdom and under-standing, the spirit of counsel and might, the spirit of knowledge and of the fear of the LORD." Here we have three couplets, which with the addition of the term, "The Spirit of the LORD", make seven descriptions of the one Spirit of God.

There was no measurement given for the Golden Candlestick, setting forth the infinite fullness of our risen Lord. Though He carried Manhood to the throne of God, never to drop it henceforth, yet there is the answer to the measureless Candlestick, "In Him dwelleth all the fullness of the Godhead bodily" (Colossians 2:9).

It is clear that the full light of God could not shine forth till Christ was raised and ascended. Wonderful as the light was when He was here on earth as the Light of the world, yet the whole truth could not come out. It was only after resurrection that the Lord could say to Mary, "Go to My brethren, and say unto them, I ascend unto My Father and your Father; and to My God and your God" (John 20:17), thus announcing the new and wondrous relationship formed by love Divine, in virtue of His death and resurrection, and by the power of the Holy Spirit.

Again it was not until Christ was in resurrection and ascended, not until He took His place on high, and the Holy Spirit descended in the full and peculiar way characteristic of Christianity, that the truth of the one body could come out, that mystery hid from all ages. "There is one body, and one Spirit, even as ye are called in one hope of your calling" (Ephesians 4:4).

The Candlestick was made of *beaten* work. Even in the glory there will ever be the remembrance and witness to the amazing love of our Lord in enduring the bruising of the cross for us. "He was *bruised* for our iniquities" (Isaiah 53:5). The Apostle John was told, "Weep not: behold the Lion of the tribe of Judah, the Root of David, hath prevailed to open the book, and to loose the seven seals thereof" (Revelation 5:5). When he looked, he saw "The Lion of the tribe of Judah", but as "a *Lamb* as it had been slain, having seven horns and seven eyes, which are the Seven Spirits of God sent forth into all the earth." And when the glorious city, symbolic of the Church in administration during the Millennium, is seen, she is introduced as "The Bride, the *Lamb's* wife" (Revelation 21:9).

There were instruments accompanying the service of the Candlestick. We read, "And the tongs thereof, and the snuff dishes thereof shall be of pure gold" (Exodus 25:38). We have spoken of the Candlestick, or Lampholder, type of Christ Himself; and the oil, type of the Holy Spirit, but no mention is made of the wick, or cotton, without which there would be no light. But the snuff dishes clearly imply this. They should be used to remove the charred portion of the wick after hours of burning, so that the light might be unhindered, and be in full strength. We cannot refer the snuffers to the Holy Spirit of God. That is clear. But we do know that the Holy Spirit uses *human* vessels through which His ministry may flow. We have the gifts—the apostles and prophets, the pastors and teachers, the helps, the joints and bands of the body of Christ.

If the Holy Spirit uses human vessels, there is room for corrective ministry, in other words the need of the snuffers. Take the case of the Apostle Peter. He was anxious to prove his devotedness to His Lord, but what self-confidence was mixed up with it. He denied His Lord with oaths and cursing. Christ graciously used his fall to teach His impetuous servant very necessary lessons. The golden snuffers were used to good effect. See how clearly the light shone on the Day of Pentecost, when he gave testimony to Christ in wonderful power, and three thousand souls were added to the Lord.

Or take the case of the Apostle Paul. Likely to be puffed up beyond measure by the wonderful things he saw and heard in the third heaven, the Lord gave him a thorn in the flesh, a messenger of Satan to buffet him. The golden snuffers did their work. The Holy Spirit strengthened Paul to do a mighty work in founding assemblies, in giving light and blessing to the whole Church of God.

Remember the Golden Candlestick held the Light

The oil, typical of the Holy Spirit, *fed* the light.

The wick, believers as used of the Spirit, *pass on* the light.

But remember, the Church does not teach. The Church is not the source of light. It is only as God's people are kept in humble communion and self-emptiness that God can use them. In the Holy City, symbolic of the Church in administration in the millennial period, we read, "The nations of them which are saved shall walk in the light of it" (Revelation 21:24). But that light is not the light of the Church. In the previous verse to the one just quoted we read, "The glory of God did lighten it, and the Lamb is the light thereof." It is the light of God and of the Lamb shining through the city that gives light to the saved nations. Unless this is clearly grasped we are in danger of mysticism.

> *"'Twas **I** did this, 'Twas **I** did that,*
> *Nay, brother, nay, take thought and say*
> *What fountain fills thy emptiness.*
> *The central wick has grown too thick,*
> *Instead of keeping spare and slim."*

Chapter 7:
The Curtains of the Tabernacle

READ **EXODUS 26:1-14**

There were four curtains or coverings for the Tabernacle:—

1. *Curtains of fine twined Linen.*

2. *Curtains of Goats' Hair.*

3. *Covering of Rams' Skins dyed red.*

4. *Covering of Badgers' Skins.*

As remarked before, the instructions as to the coverings are given before those concerning the boards. It is just these surprises that show us the beauty and accuracy of Scripture, and emphasize Divine inspiration. The coverings all speak of Christ, whereas the boards are typical of believers, "builded together for an habitation of God through the Spirit" (Ephesians 2:22). It is the full truth about Christ that enables us to understand the place and blessing the believer has in Him. Christ is the key that unlocks all doors of blessing and happiness.

The Curtains of fine twined linen constituted the *Tabernacle* [Hebrew, *Miskan*].

The Curtains of Goats' Hair constituted the *Tent*, or Covering [Hebrew, *Ohel*].

The Rams' Skins dyed red were called a *Covering* [Hebrew, *Mikseh*].

The Badgers' Skins were called a Covering [Hebrew, *Mikseh*].

NUMBERS STAMPED UPON THE CURTAINS

There were *ten* curtains, *five* curtains were looped one to the other by loops of blue; the other *five* curtains were looped one to the other by similar loops. These two *fives* were fastened together by *fifty* taches, or small hooks, made of gold. Thus it became one Covering. The reader will notice how the number *five* and its multiples are stamped upon the Curtains, speaking typically of responsibility Godward and Manward having been met by our Lord when He died upon the cross.

The length of each Curtain was *twenty-eight* cubits and their breadth *four* cubits. Twenty-eight cubits (4 x 7) by four cubits resolves each length into *seven* SQUARES of *four* cubits each. *Seven* is the number of Divine perfection, *four* sets forth that which is universal. Surely this prefigures Christ. He is the transcendent Figure of all ages. He is the One Person of universal and paramount importance in all time. Many have snatched at world-wide dominion. He alone shall reign universally, as likewise His atoning death has in view the whole world. "God so loved the world that He gave His only begotten Son" (John 3:16). Others have been great, virtuous and good, but all save our Lord have come short of perfection. He alone could be marked by what the figures *seven* and *four* typify.

THE CURTAINS OF FINE TWINED LINEN

These were the innermost curtains, furthest removed from the observer outside, the nearest to the priests, as they ministered inside. The word, Tabernacle, does not suggest anything *temporary*. The idea of the Tabernacle is a Dwelling Place, and when God chooses a Dwelling Place it is an *everlasting* choice. The Tabernacle in the wilderness was only temporary, but then it was a type, which had to pass away. What is typified is not temporary but *eternal*.

In the New Testament we find God dwelling amongst His people, and when the end of time shall have come, and the fixed eternal state reached, we find these words, "Behold the Tabernacle of God is with men, and He will dwell with them [*just as He did typically in the wilderness*], and they shall be His people, and God Himself shall be with them, and be their God" (Revelation 21:3). The Curtains were "of fine twined linen, and blue, and purple, and scarlet: with cherubims of cunning work shalt thou make them" (Exodus 26:1). Though we dealt briefly with these materials in our first chapter, we will add some further details here.

Fine twined linen typified the holy spotless Humanity of our Lord. "Let Thy priests be clothed with righteousness" (Psalm 132:9), and we know they were actually clothed in fine linen. "Fine linen is the righteousness [literally *righteousnesses*] of saints" (Revelation 19:8), is another Scripture that confirms the thought of what fine twined linen stands for, a symbol of holiness in life and walk. Christ was pre-eminently and absolutely holy in His walk.

Blue sets forth the heavenly character of our Lord's Humanity. He became a true Man when born of the Virgin at Bethlehem, but all the moral qualities of His life were heavenly in their origin. So we find the Lord saying, "And no man hath ascended up to Heaven, but He that came down from Heaven, even the Son of Man, which is in Heaven" (John 3:13). "The second Man is the Lord from Heaven" (1 Corinthians 15:47).

Purple sets forth Christ's glory as Son of Man, as King of kings and Lord of lords. Purple is the colour of the emperor. An emperor is strictly a King of kings. The ex-Emperor of Germany was Emperor in virtue of the fact that Germany embraced four kingdoms, Prussia, Saxony, Württemburg, and Bavaria. None but Christ has the right absolutely to wear the purple, and it is a joy to His people to know that He will reign universally as King of kings and Lord of lords, the true world Emperor.

> *"Outstretched His wide dominion*
> *O'er river, sea and shore.*
> *Far as the eagle's pinion,*
> *Or dove's light wing can soar."*

Scarlet is the kingly colour. The Gospel of Matthew presents Christ as the King of Israel. At the time of the crucifixion the soldiers in mockery put on Christ a *scarlet* robe, mocking Him, saying, "Hail, King of the Jews" (Matthew 27:29). Christ has been rejected by His earthly people, but He will yet reign over them as their King, their Messiah, God's anointed One.

Cherubims speak of judgment. Cherubims guarded the tree of life when our first parents were driven out of the Garden of Eden. Fire was between the cherubims in Ezekiel 10:6. When Christ, who has borne the judgment of sin at the cross, takes up the question of judgment for those who have refused His grace and love, it will be righteous judgment. There will be no miscarriage of judgment then. Every wrong will be punished, and right will be vindicated. The poet sang:

> *"Truth forever on the scaffold,*
> *Wrong forever on the throne,*
> *Yet that scaffold sways the future,*
> *And behind the dim unknown*
> *Standeth God behind the shadow,*
> *Keeping watch above His own."*

Christ will bring in the true "New Order" that men are vainly trying to introduce, leaving Him out, who alone can bring it in.

Whilst all this is true, yet the cherubims worked with cunning work on these Curtains set forth that Divine judgment has been met by our Lord at the cross of Calvary. Thus the worshipper has all the peace of a purged conscience.

How gloriously do these Curtains typify Christ in His personal purity and official glories, leaving one with a glowing sense of His perfection and triumph. He is indeed perfection, which will finally permeate to the ends of the earth, reminding us of the Scripture, "All the ends of the world shall remember and turn unto the LORD; and all the kindreds of the nations shall worship before Thee" (Psalm 22:27).

The loops of *blue* and taches of *gold* bring out the thought that everything for God, and for us, is secured on the ground of Divine righteousness (gold) and heavenly grace (blue).

THE CURTAINS OF GOATS' HAIR

As we have seen in our note in Chapter 1, goats' hair garments are typical of the prophet, so these Curtains of Goats' hair, eleven in number, and two cubits longer than the fine twined linen Curtains, set forth Christ as the Prophet. Moses prophesied of Christ in his day. "The LORD thy God will raise up unto thee a Prophet from the midst of thee, of thy brethren, like unto me; unto Him ye shall hearken" (Deuteronomy 18:15).

As the beautiful inner Curtains constituted the *Tabernacle*, so the Goats' Hair Curtains constituted the *Tent*, which speaks of that which is temporary, a wilderness provision as long as it is needed. The Tabernacle typified the universe of eternal bliss that lies ahead of every believer. Thank God, the wilderness is not for ever.

The extra Curtain with its extra length allowed for these to overlap the beautiful inner Curtains, which latter were only for the eyes of the priests in the Holy Place.

We often limit the idea of a prophet to one who foretells future events. The main idea of the prophet is that of a *forth*teller, as well as a *fore*teller. The Prophet brings his hearers into God's presence as to their state before Him. How fully Christ carried this out. "Sir, I perceive that Thou art a Prophet" (John 4:19), cried out the startled woman at the well of Sychar, as in three or four brief sentences the Lord laid bare the secrets of her guilty past. It is ever so. The prophet to be effective must reach the conscience of his hearers. The prophet, whether addressing a sinful nation, as Isaiah and others did in their day, or those, who prophesy in this dispensation (Romans 12:6), must aim at the conscience to be effective. It is true that truth enters the mind through the conscience rather than through the intellect. The intellect grasping the truth without the conscience being affected becomes "knowledge [*that*] puffeth up" (1 Corinthians 8:1).

The Covering of Rams' Skins Dyed Red

The word, Covering, is not used in connection with the curtains of fine twined linen. It is, however, specifically used for the rams' skins and the badgers' skins. The *Curtains* present Christ *personally*, the *Coverings*, *qualities* that marked Him when on earth. We shall see this clearly as we proceed.

The first mention of the ram in connection with the Tabernacle throws light on the subject. Two rams were employed on the occasion of the *consecration* of Aaron and his sons. The second Ram was slain, and its blood was not only sprinkled on the Altar round about, but it was put upon the tip of the right ear, the thumb of the right hand, the great toe of the right foot of Aaron and his sons, claiming them in their walk and ways for God. It was called *"a Ram of consecration"*. In this we learn that the Ram sets forth *consecration*, the skins dyed red, showing how far that consecration could go in the case of our Lord, even to death. This was our Lord's consecration to the will of His Father. "Then said I, Lo, I come (in the volume of the book it is written of Me) to do Thy will, O God" (Hebrews 10:7), and that led Him to the death of the cross.

This then was the motive power that carried Christ from the glory into this dark world, and maintained Him in His devoted service, and supported Him, even at the moment of sorest trial in Gethsemane's garden, where His sweat was as it were great drops of blood. He cried in bitterest anguish, "O My Father, if it be possible, let this cup pass from Me; nevertheless not as I will, but as Thou wilt" (Matthew 26:39). His will was the same as God's will, and this carried Him through the sorest trial of all, the cross itself, where consecration was exhibited to the full. Verily, the Rams' skins were *dyed red*. Precious Saviour!

THE COVERING OF BADGERS' SKINS

There has been a good deal of enquiry as to what was meant by badgers' skins. The badger is an animal unknown in Bible lands. Whatever these skins were they were common among the children of Israel, for we read, "And every man, with whom was found blue, and purple, and scarlet, and fine linen, and goats' hair, and red skins of rams, and *badgers' skins* brought them" (Exodus 35:23). The only other place where Badgers' skins are mentioned apart from this outer covering of the Tabernacle is Ezekiel 16:10, where it says, "I ... shod thee with badgers' skin", giving the idea of something coarse and durable, suitable for footwear. It is generally thought it may refer to the tough skin of the seal or dolphin, which animals are abundant in the Red Sea. Such skin would be very durable, and resist sun and rain.

The so-called badgers' skins formed the outermost covering of the Tabernacle. Does this not typify how Christ appeared to the people of Israel? Did not Isaiah prophesy centuries before He came into the world, how the world would treat Him. "He hath no form nor comeliness: and when we shall see Him, there is no beauty that we should desire Him. He is despised and rejected of men: a Man of sorrows and acquainted with grief; and we hid as it were our faces from Him; He was despised, and we esteemed Him not" (Isaiah 53:2-3).

It is tragic to see Him "the altogether lovely One", in God's estimation as "a tender plant, and as a root out of a dry ground" (Isaiah 53:2), the one Object on earth that Heaven could look upon with perfect complacency, unrecognized by man in His true character. "He was in the world, and the world was made by Him, and the world knew Him not. He came unto His own, and His own received Him not" (John 1:10-11). Such is man in his fallen estate.

Chapter 8:
The Boards of the Tabernacle

READ EXODUS 26:15-30

God's desire ever has been to dwell among His people. Thus far in the Tabernacle we have had Christ personally as the Mediator, and His work, typically before us. "There is one God, and one Mediator between God and men, the Man Christ Jesus; who gave Himself a Ransom for all, to be testified in due time" (1 Timothy 2:5-6). "Christ also hath once suffered for sins, the Just for the unjust, that *He might bring us* TO GOD" (1 Peter 3:18). We need neither the Virgin Mary, blessed among women, nor the pope, nor priest, be he Roman or Anglican, to mediate for us. The believer is brought to God, and has boldness to enter the Holiest of All by the blood of Jesus.

We shall find how the lesson of the boards will tell us typically how believers are brought to God, and "builded together for an habitation of God through the Spirit" (Ephesians 2:22). If the reader will look upon the Board as representing himself, and follow the details of what happened to the Boards, as illustrating what happened to him when converted, he will learn much of how we are blessed as believers.

THE BOARDS STANDING UP

The boards were made of shittim wood, *standing up*. Shittim wood speaks of humanity. In the case of the blessed Lord His Humanity was spotless and sinless, else He could not have taken our place at the cross. In our case we are fallen and sinful. How then in our case can the board stand up? In other words, How can a guilty sinner stand up before a holy God?

The boards were *ten* cubits high and a cubit and a half wide, that is over 17 feet high and 2½ feet wide [6]. They were made of shittim wood, the coarse indestructible wood of the desert, worth very little, but exceedingly heavy. How were they to stand up on shifting sand? Alas! how many sinners seek to stand up before God on the shifting sand of good works, and self-improvement, as if man could be his own Saviour.

The boards were *ten* cubits high. *Five* is the number of human responsibility, *ten*, twice *five*, intensifying the thought of responsibility towards God, responsibility towards man. Nowadays men do not like this thought, but there it is, spite of what men may think. "Every one of us shall give account of himself to God" (Romans 14:12).

THE SILVER SOCKETS

If the reader will turn to Exodus 30:11-16, he will find that when Israel was numbered it was necessary to furnish a ransom for their souls, failing which plague would break out upon them. King David once numbered the people, but there is no mention of their giving a ransom. The record is, "The LORD sent a pestilence upon Israel from morning even to the time appointed: and there died of the people from Dan even to Beer-sheba seventy thousand men" (2 Samuel 24:15). God cannot take account of sinful men in the flesh save in judgment. If man is to be in favour before God it must be through an accepted ransom.

All the males among the Israelites from twenty years old and upward had to bring a half shekel of silver. This contained *ten* gerahs in weight, as if to typify the meeting of the penalty of breaking the *ten* commandments, for "whosoever shall keep the whole law, and yet offend in one point, he is guilty of all" (James 2:10). A half shekel of silver was worth about one shilling and two pence [7]. However rich an Israelite was, he was not allowed to give more; however poor, he must not give less. Does this not set forth the truth that there is only one way of blessing for rich and poor, noble and debased, and that is through the atoning work of Christ upon the cross.

But we think we hear someone say, If the half shekel of silver is called "atonement money", is that not like paying for salvation? We are told in the New Testament that eternal life is the gift of God, and that we are saved by faith, and that the gift of God.

It is perfectly true that salvation can not be bought by money, nor by any effort of the sinner. It is indeed procured by the propitiation of Christ on the cross, and that is "not of works, lest any man should boast" (Ephesians 2:9).

Redemption could not be procured by a paltry levy of a sum a trifle more than a shilling. That small sum was simply an *acknowledgment* on the part of the offerer of how he stood in God's presence, needing grace and pardon.

An illustration may help. Years ago we were seeking to rent a piece of ground on which to erect a Gospel Tent. A suitable spot presented itself. On enquiry we were told it was the property of the town. We went to the Town Hall, prepared to pay £1, or even 30s. a week rent for the use of it. We found the corporation officials sympathetic, and after a little consultation they said, "We are prepared to let you have the use of the pitch for six weeks, free of rent, but as we are obliged to have some record of the transaction in our books, we must ask you for the sum of one shilling." We blessed our good fortune, but it never occurred to us that we were paying rent, but simply making an *acknowledgment*. So it was with the children of Israel.

These paltry half shekels mounted to a considerable quantity of silver when every male Israelite of twenty years old and upward paid this levy. Exodus 38:25-28 informs us it amounted to 100 talents, and 1,775 shekels. The 100 talents produced 100 sockets of silver, whilst 1,775 shekels provided the silver for the hooks for the pillars, overlaying and filleting the chapiters.

Two sockets of silver were apportioned to each board, fifty boards in all. A talent of silver weighed 114 lbs., which at 5s. an ounce amounts to over £340, so that the two sockets allotted to one board would mean silver to the value of £680. The 100 sockets for the fifty boards amounted to the sum of about £34,000 [8].

Was there ever in proportion to its size a more costly foundation? Yes, indeed, if the type was very costly, it pales into utter insignificance when we think of the redemptive work of our Lord Jesus Christ, the Son of God, dying on the cross of shame for us as the righteous foundation of the believer's standing and blessing before God. No wonder we read, "Ye know that ye were not redeemed with corruptible things, as silver and gold, from your vain conversation received by tradition from your fathers; but with the precious blood of Christ, as of a lamb without blemish and without spot" (1 Peter 1:18-19). The type was amazingly costly; the Antitype infinitely more so. All the boards of the Tabernacle stood on costly sockets of silver, the believer stands on redemption ground. Surely the hymn writer must have had this in mind:

"Oh! joyous hour when God to me
A vision gave of Calvary;
My bonds were loosed, my soul unbound;
I sang upon redemption ground.

> *Redemption ground, the ground of peace!*
> *Redemption ground, Oh! wondrous grace.*
> *Here let our praise to God abound,*
> *Who saves us on REDEMPTION GROUND."*

THE MEANING OF THE TWO TENONS

We read, "Two tenons [margin, *hands*] shall there be in one board, set in order one against another" (Exodus 26:17). Is this not an illustration of *the hand of* FAITH laying hold of the blessing? Does it not emphasize that salvation is not of *works*, but by *faith* in the atoning sacrifice of Christ? We have the hands at work in Hebrews 6:18, where it speaks of those "who have fled for refuge to *lay hold* upon the hope" set before them.

Further there were two tenons, or hands, to lay hold upon two sockets of silver, the tenon and mortise of the carpenter. One tenon, or hand, and one socket would not be so stable as two tenons to the one board with two sockets, both equally taking the strain, thus giving stability and rigidity. So in the atoning work of Christ there are two great fundamental truths presented for our acceptance:

1.   *The finished work of Christ on the cross.*

2.   *His glorious resurrection proving the acceptance of the work of redemption by God.*

Faith can triumphantly and joyously say, Christ "was delivered for our offences, and was raised again for our justification. Therefore being justified by faith [*the hands laying hold on these two great facts*], we have peace with God through our Lord Jesus Christ" (Romans 4:25; 5:1).

The resurrection proves that the atonement was completed to God's full satisfaction. It is the Divine attestation to the work of salvation wrought out on the cross. What a foundation for the believer! The finished work of Christ! A risen triumphant living Saviour!

No wonder the big heavy boards of the Tabernacle stood up well on such secure foundations as the twin silver sockets. No wonder that the believer can stand up before God in the value and efficacy of the work of our Lord on the cross, attested to by the triumph of the resurrection.

There were two extra corner boards coupled together by one ring resting on four sockets of silver, two for each board, thus emphasizing the thought of stability.

A Scriptural illustration may help further to the understanding of the two sockets. Two disciples were wending their way back to Emmaus from Jerusalem. They had placed their hopes on Christ, and now He had been crucified, had died, and this was the third day since He had been buried. There were rumours that He was risen, but there was no convincing proof that this was so, and these two disciples were left in sore doubt and depression.

Our Lord, risen from the dead, drew near to them. Their eyes were holden that they should not know Him. He enquired of their sadness. In their doubt and sadness they said, "We trusted that it had been He which should have redeemed Israel: and beside all this, to-day is the third day since these things were done" (Luke 24:21). Then followed a wonderful exposition of Scripture from the lips of the unknown Stranger, as He asked the question, "Ought not Christ to have suffered these things, and to enter into His glory" (Luke 24:26), which made their hearts burn within them, and caused them to constrain Him, saying, "Abide with us: for it is toward evening, and the day is far spent."

He graciously acceded to their wishes, and lo! they discovered that the Stranger, who had ravished their hearts by His matchless exposition of Scripture to their utmost joy, was none other than the risen Saviour, Conqueror over sin and death and hell. The scales fell from their eyes, as they beheld the risen Christ, standing before them. Did they see the nail prints in His blessed hands, we wonder, as He broke the bread at that hallowed evening meal?

For see, how unstable these disciples were when they only knew of the death of Christ. It needed the risen Christ to convince them of the value of that wondrous work upon the cross. His death acquired a far greater and fuller meaning in the light of His resurrection, as they stood with wondrous joy and delight in His very presence.

One moment He stood revealed before them, the next moment He had vanished out of their sight. But no more doubt now. The boards were secure on the two sockets of silver apiece. The hands of faith, like the two tenons laid hold with a firm grip upon the grand foundation. Thus would God assure our poor unbelieving hearts.

THE BOARDS FITLY JOINED TOGETHER

We have hitherto considered each board as an individual board. We shall, however, not get a proper idea of what

God had in view unless we see that the board was intended to be an integral part of the whole Tabernacle. It was never intended to remain a single board "standing up". It was intended to be put into juxtaposition with the other boards, twenty boards on the south side, twenty on the north side, two boards for the corners of the Tabernacle, six boards for the west side (Exodus 26:22-25), and four pillars with four sockets for the hanging of the vail between the Holy Place and the Holiest of All, making 100 sockets in all, necessary for their foundation.

What did this all typify? We have proceeded from the individual board to the boards "fitly joined together". What did it signify? We answer, God would have a people among whom He might dwell, a spot where He can place His name. This was set forth typically in the Tabernacle.

When we come to the New Testament we find the anti-type to this. The boards were fitly joined together. We read, "Now therefore ye are no more strangers and foreigners, but fellow-citizens with the saints, and of the household of God: and are BUILT upon the foundation of the apostles and prophets, Jesus Christ Himself being the chief Corner Stone" (Ephesians 2:19-20). Again, "In whom ye also are BUILDED together for an habitation of God through the Spirit" (Ephesians 2:22). Again, "Ye also, as lively stones, are BUILT up a spiritual house, an holy priesthood, to offer up spiritual sacrifices, acceptable to God by Jesus Christ" (1 Peter 2:5). God has a house here on earth composed or built up of His own redeemed people, among whom He is pleased to dwell. How good it is that believers are not saved to remain as individuals, that there is a wonderful Christian fellowship, likened to a building, reared up by the Holy Spirit of God. How we should prize such fellowship. It is indeed a source of strength and encouragement when God's people get together as gathered to the Lord by the Holy Spirit. So we read of the early disciples, that "they continued steadfastly in the apostles' doctrine and FELLOWSHIP, and in breaking of bread and in prayers" (Acts 2:42).

THE FIVE BARS

When the boards were placed in position, on either side of the Tabernacle were placed five horizontal bars. At the bottom of the boards there ran two bars, at the top were two bars, whilst an unusual arrangement was made for the middle bar. We read, "And the middle bar in *the* MIDST *of the boards* shall reach from end to end" * (Exodus 26:28), that is, it was grooved out of sight. Nothing could have been designed to clamp and bind more strongly together the boards. Thus a compact structure was ensured.

What did the four visible bars typify? We believe they set forth the gifts given by an ascended Lord to His Church. What in particular did the two bars at the bottom of the boards typify? We believe the answer is that the Church is "built upon the FOUNDATION of the Apostles and Prophets, Jesus Christ Himself being the chief Corner Stone" (Ephesians 2:20). We get it in symbolic language, "And the wall of the city [*the Church in Millennial administration*] had twelve FOUNDATIONS, and in them the names of the twelve Apostles of the Lamb" (Revelation 21:14). How indebted we are to the Apostles and Prophets for the introduction of Christianity in this world, in their labours in forming assemblies, and in their inspired writings.

The Apostle John, associating the rest of the Apostles in his statement, wrote, "That which we have seen and heard declare we unto you, that ye also may have fellowship

---

* The Revised Version renders Exodus 26:28, "and the middle bar in the midst of the boards shall *pass through* from end to end."

with us: and truly our fellowship is with the Father, and with His Son Jesus Christ. And these things write we unto you, that your joy may be full" (1 John 1:3-4). How wonderful was that fellowship, first of all their acquaintance with Christ drawing each Apostle to the other, then the passing of it on to us, drawing believers to Christ and to their fellow believers.

We must remember these Prophets were *New Testament* Prophets, and had a unique position in revealing the mind of God to the Christians in the days of the early Church. This is seen in the memorable chapter on the edification, or building up, of the Church as seen in 1 Corinthians 14:29-31.

What was the meaning of the two bars at the top of the boards? We believe they set forth those wonderful gifts to the Church, Pastors and Teachers. These were given "for the perfecting of the saints, for the work of the ministry, for the edifying of the body of Christ" (Ephesians 4:12). The evangelist does not come in here as an evangelist. His gift is with the wide world and sinners, and very blessed is his service in this way. But his converts need to be shepherded in the things of the Lord by the pastor. The word for shepherd and pastor is the same in the original. Then comes the teacher to unfold the deep things of God's word, whereby to build up the Lord's people in their faith. The pastor is like the nurse. Did not the Apostle Paul write, "We were gentle among you, even as a nurse cherisheth her children" (1 Thessalonians 2:7)? The teacher is more like the schoolmaster.

But what is the meaning of the long bar out of sight, the binding bar, grooved and tongued throughout the boards from end to end? What typical meaning attaches to this bar? We have no doubt that this bar typifies the Holy

Spirit of God in His *unseen* power and influence. Without the influence of God's Holy Spirit, actively at work among the believers, there would be no cohesion, no standing together. Where that power and influence is weak or absent, there will be disunion, divisions, parties, sects. But where the Spirit of God is present *in power*, there the Lord's people will be found walking in peace and unity. The body of Christ was formed on the Day of Pentecost, when the Holy Spirit came to indwell each believer, binding them each first of all to Christ, the Head of the body in Heaven, and to each other on earth as members of the one body. "There is one body, and one Spirit", and we are called upon to be found "endeavouring to keep *the unity of the* SPIRIT in the bond of peace" (Ephesians 4:3-4).

THE BOARDS OVERLAID WITH GOLD

Finally, instructions are given to overlay the boards with gold, to provide rings of gold for the bars, and overlay the bars with gold. Here as the boards typify believers, the gold cannot set forth Deity. It sets forth the *Divine righteousness* in which the believer stands before God.

That this is no arbitrary interpretation is seen in the fact that shittim wood and PURE *gold* set forth the Humanity and Deity of our Lord, whereas in this case, when it refers typically to believers, it is shittim wood and *gold*, without the adjective pure. Further in the case of shittim wood and PURE gold in connection with the Ark and Shewbread Table, the instructions for the overlaying of the shittim wood with *pure* gold follow immediately, whereas in the present case the instructions for the making of the boards of shittim wood begin in Exodus 26:15, and not till verse 29 is reached are instructions given for the overlaying of the boards with gold. Between these two points, fourteen verses in all, the instructions as to the silver sockets (redemption) are given.

Does this not convey the thought that the believer enters into the knowledge of the forgiveness of sins (*silver*) first, and that righteousness (*gold*), with which justification is connected so very manifestly, is entered into as the full meaning of the death of Christ is grasped? At the same time, let it be clearly stated, the moment the sinner believes, he gets forgiveness of sins, justification, the righteousness of God upon Him, at one and the same moment, even when he puts his faith in the Lord Jesus as Saviour. But whilst this is so, we go a step at a time in our understanding and appreciation of these things.

Young believer, look at those upright boards, and see in type what God would have you to know and enjoy. They then stand ten cubits high, speaking of responsibility to God, but they stand in silver sockets (redemption); the two tenons, or hands, grasping the foundation firmly, in other words, salvation is *by faith alone;* they are covered with gold (*Divine righteousness, the answer to the atoning death of our Lord*), typifying the justification the believer receives the moment he believes on the Lord Jesus Christ in simple faith as his Saviour and Lord. So we read of "the righteousness of God, which is by faith of Jesus Christ unto all, and UPON [typically *boards covered by gold*] all them that believe" (Romans 3:22). "Christ Jesus, who of God is made unto us ... RIGHTEOUSNESS" (1 Corinthians 1:30).

We remember the case of an English nobleman, who had been converted out and out. He read the word of God with great eagerness. One winter's day amid the snows of Canada, riding at the head of his troops, the verse came to his mind, "Thy righteousness also, O God, is very high, who hast done great things: O God, who is like unto Thee" (Psalm 71:19). This Scripture came in great power to his soul. He exclaimed to himself with great joy, "Then *I* am as high as God's righteousness."

If Christ is our righteousness as believers, can we better that? Nay, the convert of yesterday is as righteous in God's sight as the Apostle Paul in the glory. The youngest believer has this gift in all its fullness, the maturest saint cannot have it in larger measure. Rejoice, young believer, God's righteousness is upon you in virtue of Christ's work of redemption on the cross.

In human law courts it is impossible in strict justice to justify the guilty. But such is the efficacy of the work of Christ on the cross, so thoroughly has He taken our place of judgment there, that God is able *to justify the* UNGODLY. We read, "To him that worketh not, but believeth on Him *that justifieth the* UNGODLY, his faith is counted for righteousness" (Romans 4:5).

The fact of God's righteousness being upon the believing sinner is portrayed in parabolic language in Luke 15, where we read that when the prodigal returned to the father in his rags and misery, the father cried out in the gladness of his heart, "Bring forth *the best robe*, and put it on him, and put a ring on his hand, and shoes on his feet: and bring hither the fatted calf, and kill it; and let us eat and be merry" (Luke 15:22-23). The righteousness of God by faith of Jesus Christ UPON all believers is surely "the best robe".

Justification is the believer being seen in the presence of God blameless, as if he had never sinned at all. Reader, do you rejoice in this marvellous blessing? Nothing less than this would suit God's presence and pleasure.

Chapter 9:
The Vail and the Hanging for the Door of the Tent

READ **EXODUS 26:31-37**

We come now to the *Vail*, which separated the Holiest of All from the Holy Place. It typified Christ. It was made of blue, and purple and scarlet, and fine twined linen of cunning work, with cherubims worked upon it. We need not dwell on the meaning of these colours, as we have already considered them in connection with the Curtains of the Tabernacle. But we may notice a difference in the order in which the items are presented, in that here the blue came first, and the fine twined linen came last with an added description of "cunning work". The blue coming first emphasized the fact that Christ is the Heavenly One, leading His people into *Heavenly* things, whilst the fine twined linen spoke of the spotless humanity of our Lord, "the cunning work", that all the details and minutiæ of that life will only afford the reverent believer delight and pleasure. The cherubims worked on the Vail signify that all judgment is committed to the Son, who will carry out righteous judgment, and also that judgment is *past* for the believer, because Christ has borne the penalty of sin fully.

When judgment is carried out the saints of God will rejoice. This is seen when the great whore, apostate Christendom, is judged, as seen in Revelation 19:2-4. The smoke of her torment rises up for ever and ever, and we find the four and twenty elders, symbolizing the saints, who have part in the first resurrection, worshipping and saying, "Amen; Alleluia." It is only those, who are in glory past all judgment on the ground of the atoning work of Christ, who can enter rightly into such solemn scenes.

The Vail was hung upon four pillars of shittim wood over-laid with gold. Four speaks of what is universal. God has in mind the blessing of all, who will come through Christ.

The hooks of the pillars were of gold, and the sockets of silver, thus showing that it is only on the ground of redemption (silver), and righteousness (gold) that God can have to do with men.

Hebrews 10:19-22 tells us most beautifully what the Vail symbolized. "Having therefore, brethren, boldness to enter into the Holiest by the blood of Jesus, by a new and living way, which He hath consecrated for us, through the Veil, that is to say, His flesh: and having an High Priest over the house of God; let us draw near with a true heart in full assurance of faith, having our hearts sprinkled from an evil conscience, and our bodies washed with pure water."

The High Priest could only go into the Holiest of All with much solemnity on the Great Day of Atonement. He went in with the blood of bulls and goats, which could never put away sin, for his action was only typical. That being so the Vail remained. No footfall was heard in the Holiest of All for another full year, till the Day of Atonement came round, and the same ritual was gone through, and the Vail still remained up. "Into the second [*the Holiest of All*] went the High Priest alone once every year, not without blood, which he offered for himself, and for the errors of the people: the Holy Ghost this signifying, that the way into the Holiest of All was not yet made manifest, while as the first Tabernacle was yet standing" (Hebrews 9:7-8).

But in the Antitype, Christ is both Sacrifice and offering Priest. Though He could not be a priest on earth, because He did not belong to the tribe of Levi, yet He performed a priestly act when He laid down His life on the cross as a Sacrifice for sin. It must have been a moment of all moments when He cried with a loud voice, "IT IS FINISHED", the wonderful, amazing work of atonement, the only hope of the world's redemption, completed. Even very nature gave witness at that moment, for the earth did quake and the rocks were rent, the very forces of the material world were convulsed, and above all and beyond all THE VAIL WAS RENT FROM THE TOP TO THE BOTTOM, from *God's* side, by *God's* hand. What a testimony that the day of shadows was over, the day of "good things to come" had arrived. Only the High Priest could enter into the Holiest of All, and that only once a year. To-day believers have boldness of access at all times.

THE HANGING FOR THE DOOR OF THE TENT

The hanging for the Door of the Tent was of blue, and purple, and scarlet and fine twined linen, wrought with needlework. There is no need to comment on these as they have been already explained. But there is one omission worthy of careful notice. There were cherubims on the Vail between the Holiest of All and the Holy Place, but on the Door of the Tent there were no cherubims worked. By this omission God would testify that He approached man in pure sovereign grace. No cherubims, speaking of justice and judgment, were visible to the outside to affright the timid seeker after God.

> *"No curse of law, in Thee was sovereign grace,*
> *And now what glory in Thine unveiled face!*
> *Thou didst attract the wretched and the weak,*
> *Thy joy the wand'rers and the lost to seek."*

It is when God's long-suffering will have drawn to a close, that judgment will have its course, and all God's people will worship Him, because of the righteousness of His ways in judgment. But meanwhile the attitude of God to man is one of purest grace.

Five pillars supported the hanging, the pillars were of shittim wood covered with gold, hooks were of gold, the sockets of brass. This hanging spoke of man going in to God, it was the entrance for the priests as they entered upon their Sanctuary service. *Five* speaks of responsibility being met through the sacrifice of our Lord (the sockets of brass), and in consonance with righteousness (gold hooks).

Chapter 10:
The Brazen Altar

READ **EXODUS 27:1-8**

We step outside now, and find ourselves in the Court that enclosed the Tabernacle. Passing through the entrance of the Court from the outside, the first thing that met the gaze was the Brazen Altar. It was an arresting figure. A comparison between the measurement of the Ark and the Brazen Altar is interesting.

THE ARK	THE BRAZEN ALTAR
2½ cubits long	*5 cubits long*
1½ cubits broad	*5 cubits broad*
1½ cubits high	*3 cubits high*

It will be seen that the Brazen Altar was much larger than the Ark, and twice its height. God would impress upon men the necessity of atonement, if He has to do with sinful men in blessing. Would that this lesson were burned more deeply in every heart.

Unlike the Ark and Table of Shewbread, which were made of shittim wood covered with *pure gold*, the Brazen Altar was made of shittim wood, covered with *brass*. Brass, or more correctly copper, is the most fire-resisting of all the metals. The ancients had some process for hardening copper to a very high degree, the secret of which is unknown to-day. Brass (or copper) sets forth the fierceness of God's wrath against sin. "Is it nothing to you, all ye that pass by? behold, and see if there be any sorrow like unto My sorrow, which is done unto Me, wherewith the LORD hath afflicted Me in THE DAY OF HIS FIERCE ANGER" (Lamentations 1:12). As another [W. Kelly] has said, "*Gold* is the righteousness of God for drawing near where *God* is; *brass*, the righteousness of God for dealing with man's evil where *man* is."

The Brazen Altar was the place where the sacrifices were offered, the Burnt Offerings and Peace Offerings. The hands of the offerer were placed on the head of the Sacrifice, and the Sacrifice killed by the offerer, and its blood sprinkled by the priests upon the Altar.

The size of the Brazen Altar was arresting, as if God would make it very plain that there can be no approach to Him save through an atoning sacrifice. "Without shedding of blood is NO remission" (Hebrews 9:22). Further, the Brazen Altar was *foursquare*, setting forth that the Gospel message is for the whole world, north, south, east, west, for Jew and Gentile, to white, red, copper and black skins; to princes and beggars; to learned and ignorant; to religious and irreligious, to rich and poor; to young and old. So our Lord's instructions were, "Go ye into ALL the world, and preach the Gospel to EVERY creature" (Mark 16:15).

The four horns upon the Altar, made of shittim wood covered by brass, symbolize the strength of the Altar. It is as if God would assure the heart of the one, who seeks to get right with Him. We remember how Joab, fearing the result of his treachery to King Solomon, "fled unto the

Tabernacle of the LORD, and caught hold on the horns of the Altar" (1 Kings 2:28). He thought he had got to a safe asylum, but He did not come with sacrifice and blood, and the Altar was against him, and he died.

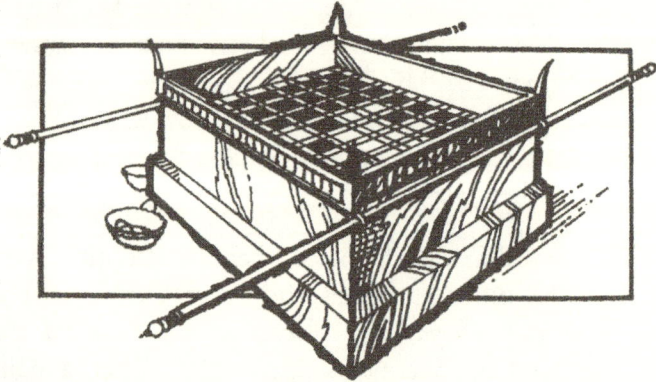

The pans, shovels, basins, flesh-hooks, firepans pertaining to the Brazen Altar, were all made of *brass*, typically showing that God will not allow us to get away from the thoughts of His holiness, His righteousness, His claims. These are met only by what the sacrifice on the Altar typifies.

A grate of network of brass was made, which fastened to four rings in the four corners of the Altar, was so placed, that the net should be held securely in the midst of the Altar. There was thus to be no escape for the victim. Right in the heart of the Altar the sacrifice was securely placed, there to be consumed by the fire.

We remember when Abraham was bidden by God to sacrifice his son upon the altar on Mount Moriah, that just as the knife was held aloft to descend quickly to do its deadly work, God graciously held back Abraham's hand, and told him there was a ram caught in the thicket by its horns, which he could slay instead of Isaac. But when our

Lord was placed upon the cross, there was no substitute for Him, no escape from the ordeal of the cross.

In the garden of Gethsemane the Lord Jesus cried out in bitterest anguish of soul, sweat like drops of blood falling to the ground, "O My Father, if it be possible, let this cup pass from Me" (Matthew 26:39), but there was no escape for Him, if atonement were to be made, which none but He could accomplish. He alone could do the mighty work. In His perfection He would add, "Nevertheless not as I will, but as Thou wilt." The network of brass was indeed a reality.

A striking attestation to all this is found in Numbers 16. When Korah, Dathan and Abiram rebelled against the priesthood, Moses instructed the rebels and Aaron his brother, to take their censers, and incense and fire, and come before the Door of the Tabernacle of the congregation. God soon answered their presumption by causing a new thing to happen, the earth opened her mouth and swallowed the rebels alive. Fire came from the Lord and consumed the two hundred and fifty men, who had offered incense. Moses then said to Eleazar, "Take up the censers out of the burning, and scatter thou the fire yonder; for they are hallowed. The censers of these sinners against their own souls, let them make them broad plates for a covering of the Altar; for they offered them before the LORD, therefore they are hallowed; and they shall be a sign unto the children of Israel" (Numbers 16:37-38).

The censers beaten into broad plates, placed as a covering on the Altar, were ever the solemn sign that God could only be approached in the way of His own ordering. There are multitudes to-day, who perish "in the gainsaying of Core [*Korah*]" (Jude 11). Think of the Seventh Day Adventists, Millennial Dawnists, Jehovah's Witnesses,

Christian Scientists, Christadelphians, and the like, who are travelling on this deluded path with its terrible end of eternal punishment. Think of those, who teach the Mohammedan notion that death in battle saves.

Look at those censers, beaten into broad plates for a covering of the Brazen Altar, and think of the end of the men who dared to come into God's presence other than by His appointed way. Let there be no weakening of the truth of the absolute necessity for the one and only Sacrifice, that has sufficed for the meeting of God's claims.

Finally, staves of shittim wood, overlaid with brass, remind us of the wilderness character of this present time. Thank God, the wilderness is not for ever. The Father's house lies invitingly before each believer on the Lord Jesus Christ.

Chapter 11:
The Court of the Tabernacle

READ **EXODUS 27:9-19**

The number *five* and its multiples in a specially striking way are stamped upon the Court of the Tabernacle. The fine linen hangings were *five* cubits high, their length southward *one hundred* cubits, and their pillars *twenty*: their length northward *one hundred* cubits and their pillars *twenty*: their breadth westward *fifty* cubits and their pillars *ten*. So there was between each pillar a square of linen, measuring *five* cubits by *five*.

These squares of fine linen set forth what the life of our Lord was in all its purity and holiness. The pillars filleted with *silver*, with hooks of *silver* and sockets of *brass* typify, that unless the claims of God's holiness had been met at the cross, there would have been no presentation of the wonderful life of our Lord in testimony in this world. "This is He that came by water and blood, even Jesus Christ, not by water only, but by water and BLOOD" (1 John 5:6).

The total length of the hanging is significant:

100	cubits northward
100	cubits southward
50	cubits westward
30	cubits eastward
280	cubits in all

This, you may remember, was the length of the beautiful inner curtains, which were only for the eyes of the priests. The hanging of pure linen emphasizes to the whole camp the testimony of the purity of our Lord's life. There was thus no discrepancy between His outward life and inward life. When He was asked, "Who art Thou?" He could reply, "Even the Same that I said unto you from the beginning" (John 8:25). What is the difference between the Badgers' Skins Covering and the Hanging of pure white linen? The answer is, that the former is what unbelieving *man* saw in His life; the latter, the purity in which *He presented Himself* to the world. Man saw "no beauty that they should desire Him." Surely His unique manhood should have arrested their attention. "Never man spake like this Man" (John 7:46), testified the officers of the Chief Priests and Pharisees, who had been sent to take Him, but who were disarmed by His testimony, and returned empty-handed. The people "wondered at the gracious words which proceeded out of His mouth" (Luke 4:22). Alas! that men generally refused this wonderful testimony.

THE GATE OF THE COURT

The fifty cubits of the hanging with its ten pillars were apportioned in the following order:—

15	cubits and	3	pillars
20	cubits and	4	pillars
15	cubits and	3	pillars
50	cubits and	10	pillars

We notice again the multiples of *five* that obtain so strikingly. The *four* pillars allowed for the Gate of the Court are interesting, as setting forth that its Entrance was for the whole world, not for one nation, or one family, the priests, but for the wide world, wherever man is found. The Hanging of the Gate of the Court was more than the fine twined linen, it was "wrought with needlework", and had blue and scarlet and purple. We already have seen what this signifies.

The Door of the Court is typical of Christ, who said, "I *am* THE DOOR" (John 10:9). "I *am* THE WAY" (John 14:6). "There is one God, and ONE MEDIATOR between God and men, the Man, Christ Jesus" (1 Timothy 2:5). "*There is* NONE OTHER NAME under heaven, given among men, whereby we must be saved" (Acts 4:12). "No man cometh unto the Father, but by Me" (John 14:6), are His own words. Not through tears, prayers, strivings, feelings or making the supreme sacrifice on the battlefield, but through CHRIST ALONE, and in virtue of His atoning death upon the cross.

Five and its multiples speak of responsibility being met, for the pillars that supported the Hanging of fine linen were socketed in *brass*, speaking of the atoning death of our Lord. The blue, purple and scarlet speak of His personal and official glories. No cherubims were worked on the Gate of the Court. No threat, no judgment marked the Entrance. Pure sovereign grace alone is presented in the typical meaning of this beautiful Gate.

There was *only* ONE Entrance for all; *only* ONE Entrance into the Holy Place for the priests; *only* ONE Entrance into the Holiest of All for the High Priest.

THE PINS AND CORDS

If the white linen of the Court sets forth Christ primarily in His spotless life of testimony, in a secondary way it tells the believer that he should be a testimony to Christ in this world. Alas! how many of us break down in our everyday life, and forget that righteousness is not measured by paying twenty shillings in the pound[9], but in acting towards others in the grace in which we have been set up by God.

In this secondary connection the pins and cords set forth that we cannot testify in our own strength. Just as the pillars were held up by a power outside themselves, so the believer can only be upheld in testimony in the power of God's Holy Spirit.

Chapter 12:
The Garments of Glory and Beauty

READ EXODUS 28:1-39

So far in our studies we have been travelling from the inside to the outside, from the Ark in the Holiest of All to the Court of the Tabernacle. God came *out to man* in the person of His beloved Son, man goes *in to God* through Christ as the High Priest of our profession. We are bidden to "consider the Apostle and High Priest of our profession, Christ Jesus" (Hebrews 3:1). We begin now to consider how man goes in *to God* as a worshipper.

An enquirer at this stage may ask why no mention has been made of the Golden Altar in the Holy Place, and the Brazen Laver in the Court of the Tabernacle. It looks like an omission. But as we have already pointed out the reason is very beautiful. What the infidel would joyfully point out as a mistake in a fallible book, the spiritual mind can see as the plain marks of inspiration in an infallible Book.

The answer is this, Until the High Priest is in *His* place for the believer, there can be no going in to God. The Brazen

Laver had to do with the priests washing their hands and feet from defilement in the water of the Brazen Laver, so as to be clean in their Sanctuary Service. The Golden Altar was where the priests burned incense unto the Lord, typifying the worship and intercession of God's people. So now our attention will be concentrated on Aaron as a type of the Lord Jesus, as the true High Priest.

"HOLY GARMENTS ... FOR GLORY AND BEAUTY"

We have now to consider the garments of glory and beauty worn by Aaron. Christ is called "A *great* High Priest" (Hebrews 4:14). Aaron was never so called. The Antitype far surpasses the type. Whilst Aaron is a remarkable type of Christ, he stands in vivid contrast to Him in certain ways. It is anticipating, but it would be well to point out how Aaron stands in contrast to our Lord.

The fact is, that God had to take account of Aaron's *real* condition. He was a man, sinful and failing, though a High Priest. On the great day of the Consecration of Aaron and his Sons, a Sin Offering was necessary for himself and his sons. That could not be typical of our Lord, for He needed no Sin Offering. He was Himself the Sin Offering on the cross for us, which He could never have been had He needed a Saviour for Himself.

Again on the Great Day of Atonement Aaron went in twice into the Holiest of All to sprinkle the blood of the Sin Offering upon and before the Mercy Seat, first for himself, and then for the people. His first entrance for himself could not typify our Lord, for He never needed a Sin Offering for Himself. But when Aaron went in the second time to offer for the sins of the people, he was clearly a type of our Lord, for "neither by the blood of goats and calves, but by His own blood He entered in *once* into the Holy Place, having obtained eternal redemption for us" (Hebrews 9:12).

Again, Aaron and his sons had to wash their hands and feet in the water of the Brazen Laver to remove the defilement that was upon them before they entered the Holy Place to carry out their Service. Though Aaron was cleansed and forgiven through the precious blood (typically), yet he was capable of contracting defilement, and needed cleansing by water. In this he is most clearly not a type of our Lord, but stands in contrast to Him, who never was defiled as He passed through a defiling scene.

Bearing such contrasts in mind, we shall see that Aaron is in many ways a beautiful type of our Lord.

The expression High Priest implies priests. The character of our Lord as High Priest determines the believers' position and portion as priests. Exodus 28 devotes no less than thirty-nine verses descriptive of the High Priest's garments of glory and beauty, and only four verses descriptive of the garments of the priests.

Does this not teach us a lesson of very prime importance? To get a proper understanding of our place and portion as priests, that is as worshippers, it is a first necessity that we understand the Person, place and portion of our great High Priest. Once we understand somewhat His place and portion, we can more easily understand our own. Our place and portion take their character from His.

Let us now examine in detail the garments of the High Priest. They were

1. *The Breast Plate.*
2. *The Ephod.*
3. *The Robe.*
4. *The Broidered Coat.*

5. *The Mitre.*
6. *The Girdle.*
7. *The Plate* of pure gold with "Holiness to the Lord" engraved upon it.

To these were added the garments of the priests, which were

8. *Coats.*
9. *Girdles.*
10. *Bonnets.*
11. *Linen Breeches* for Aaron and his Sons.

As we examine the typical meaning of these various articles of dress, let us remember that God Himself designed them, and that wise-hearted men were raised up of God

to help in the work of producing them. Bezaleel was specially called to be the leader and director of this work. God "filled him with the Spirit of God, in wisdom, in understanding, and in knowledge, and in all manner of workmanship" (Exodus 35:31, *et seq*). How wonderful that God should inspire the execution of these garments as well as Himself planning them. Surely they must have very special lessons for us.

THE EPHOD

The word, *Ephod*, is a pure Hebrew word, meaning to "put on", and in this connection has acquired a technical meaning, and stands in the Scriptures characteristically for the priestly garment. "Did I choose him out of all the tribes of Israel to be My priest, to offer upon Mine Altar, to burn incense, to wear a*n ephod before Me?*" (1 Samuel 2:28).

"And they shall make the ephod of gold, of blue, and of purple, of scarlet, and fine twined linen, with cunning work." This list is striking in one particular. *Gold* is mentioned for the first time in addition to blue and purple and scarlet, which we saw were the colours on the innermost Curtain. Never before do we read of *gold*, as being part of any garment or hanging. Why then is *gold* mentioned?

Gold, as the golden wire-thread sparkled on the dress of the High Priest, would remind us that Christ takes His place righteously (gold, *Divine righteousness*) as our great High Priest. His High Priesthood is founded on His redemptive work, truly a firm foundation. Understanding this there is rest of heart and conscience in the knowledge that our relationship with our Lord has for its basis and foundation the glorious work of righteousness He accomplished on the cross for our salvation.

Blue speaks of the Heavenly character of our Lord's Manhood. He did not become Man till born of the Virgin Mary at Bethlehem. Yet He could say of Himself, "No man hath ascended up to heaven, but He that came down from heaven, even the Son of Man which is in heaven" (John 3:13). "The second Man is the Lord from heaven" (1 Corinthians 15:47).

Purple sets forth our Lord's glory as the Son of Man with widest dominion, as King of kings and Lord of lords, the true world Emperor.

Scarlet sets forth our Lord's glory as the King of Israel, as the Messiah of His earthly people.

Fine twined linen sets forth our Lord's spotless life. "With cunning work" brings before the delighted affections of the renewed mind all the beautiful details of that life of all lives. So we read, "For such an High Priest became us, who is holy, harmless, undefiled, separate from sinners, and made higher than the heavens" (Hebrews 7:26).

THE CURIOUS GIRDLE OF THE EPHOD

This was made of the same material as the ephod. There is no need to repeat what we said of the colours in their typical teaching, as we have just pointed these out.

But we must say a little as to the girdle itself. "Curious girdle" is an expression only used in connection with the ephod of the High Priest, and signifies devised work. It stands as a symbol of service. For instance, our blessed Lord after the Passover Supper was ended, "took a towel, and *girded* Himself. After that He poureth water into a basin, and began to wash the disciples' feet, and to wipe them with the towel wherewith He was girded" (John 13:4-5). Again we read, "Blessed are those servants, whom the Lord when He cometh shall find watching; verily I say unto you, that He shall gird Himself, and make them to sit down to meat, and will come forth and serve them" (Luke 12:37).

How touching it is to know that the Lord on high is constantly serving His people. He serves us, but most emphatically He is not our Servant, for a servant is bidden to do this or that at the command of the master. If I were bidden to the King's table, and he graciously with his own hand brought me a cup of tea, he would be serving me, but he would be very surprised, if he were told, that I had said he was my servant. The Lord's service for us is voluntary, and dictated by the love of His heart, and is showered upon His people. He serves us as the Captain of our salvation, leading us to glory; as our High Priest in connection with our infirmities and weaknesses; as our Advocate, even when a believer occasions by an act of sin the sorrowful yet faithful exercise of that office. The "Curious girdle" is typical of the service our blessed Lord renders His own. How we adore such a Saviour and render to Him our heartfelt thanks.

THE SHOULDER PLATES

These are not mentioned separately in verse 4, where we have the different articles of the High Priest's garments enumerated. They were evidently part of the ephod, and linked on with the breastplate to which they were firmly attached by wreathen chains of gold.

Two onyx stones were engraved with the names of the children of Israel, six names on one stone and six on the other. These two onyx stones were then set in ouches, or sockets, of gold, and put upon the shoulders of the ephod, Aaron thus bearing their names before the Lord for a memorial. What typical meaning has this for us in this dispensation? In Scripture the shoulder is the place of power. We read, "Unto us a child is born, unto us a Son is given: and the government shall be upon His shoulder" (Isaiah 9:6). *One* shoulder suffices for the government of the world, but when it is a question of Christ maintaining His people in the presence of God, we have *two* shoulders mentioned. Thus God would teach us how the Lord Jesus in all His ascended power is able to maintain each one of His own in the presence of God. "Christ is … entered … into Heaven itself, now to appear in the presence of God for us" (Hebrews 9:24).

We get the same thought in the parable of the Shepherd finding the lost sheep. When the Good Shepherd, symbolical of our Lord, was successful in his search, we read, "And when he hath found it, he layeth it on his *shoulders*, rejoicing" (Luke 15:5). We believers are well cared for indeed.

THE BREASTPLATE OF JUDGMENT

But this is not all. If the shoulder plates set forth the Lord's *power* exercised on our behalf, so the breastplate sets forth His *affection* for His own. It was made of the same materials as the ephod, emphasizing afresh the personal and official glories of our Lord. In this breastplate were settings of four rows of precious stones, three in each row, having engraved upon them the names of the twelve children of Israel. What the special meaning of each stone is, we are not competent to say. That they have a special significance we doubt not. A celebrated lapidary, an expert in precious stones, gave it as his considered opinion that the order in which these gems were chosen and arranged was beyond human skill, that it could only have been done by Divine arrangement.

Each precious stone had its particular character in colour, density, powers of refraction and the like, so that each precious stone was different from the others. Even so God takes account of the different ways that Divine character is produced in believers. God surely is not the Author of a mass production of articles that do not vary in the slightest degree. It is said in nature that not two blades of grass are alike, and one never sees two faces exactly alike in every particular. So doubtless it is so in the realm of grace.

The symbolic City in Revelation 21, the church symbolized in its administrative display in the millennial reign of Christ, had twelve precious stones in its foundation. As we read our New Testaments we are conscious of the difference between Paul and Peter and John and other servants of Christ. They shine on earth each in his own characteristic, reflecting the life of Christ in them in their earthly circumstances. Shall they cease to shine as "one star differeth from another star in glory"? (1 Corinthians 15:41). We think not.

But this much is plain. These precious stones, gleaming in the breastplate of the High Priest, typify our great High Priest, the Lord Jesus Christ, representing and maintaining His own in deepest affection in the presence of God. We are not lost in a crowd. We are not lumped together in a vague generality. We are each of us, individually known, cared for, ministered to, upheld, represented in all the strength of Divine love in the presence of God.

Further, rings of gold were attached to the two ends of the breastplate, and two rings were attached to the ephod, and rings were bound to rings by a lace, or riband of blue. Thus securely attached to the person of the High Priest were these precious stones. In the shoulder plates the onyx stones were set in ouches, or sockets, of gold. In the breastplate the precious stones were set in gold in their inclosing or fillings. Thus securely were the shoulder plates attached to the ephod, as also was the breastplate. With such wealth of detail would the Spirit of God emphasize the glorious truth of how Divine love and Divine power are united in the security of the believer, and their maintenance before God in Divine favour. Our Lord plainly said, "My sheep hear My Voice, and I know them, and they follow Me: and I give unto them eternal life; and they shall never perish" (John 10:27-28). Eternal life could not be given, if it could be lost. Interpose the fraction of a second, or the breadth of a hair, in interruption of eternal life, and it could not be eternal. And "never perish" means not to perish for one moment, not to perish for ever.

The reader will pardon the writer, if he gives an incident, connected with this subject, very dear to him. It was told him as a child by his sainted mother. Many years ago Charles Stanley, a gifted preacher of commanding and attractive personal appearance, stood up to preach in a large North of England city. The grandfather of the writer borrowed a chair from a near-by shop for the preacher to stand upon. Soon a large crowd assembled. As the preacher proceeded he used as a happy illustration of the security of the believer in Christ, the subject we have in hand. He spoke of the believers thus:—

"As jewels on His breast
Jesus doth ever bear."

He was speaking in a district where the doctrine was rife that a believer may be saved to-day and lost to-morrow, saved almost up to the very gate of Heaven, and yet lost at the finish. Mr. Stanley used the striking expression, "Thank God, He has no hook-and-eye believers, hooked on to-day and hooked off to-morrow." Expatiating on this happy theme that Aaron's breastplate spoke of Christ's unchanging love for His own; that the rings of gold set forth Divine righteousness; that the riband, or lace, of blue set forth heavenly grace, he stressed the absolute security of the believer. My mother often told me how she heard the subdued comments of warm approval on the part of the audience.

Then the precious stones, whether on the shoulder plates, or breastplate, were *engraved*. God said of Zion, "Behold, I have *graven* thee upon the palms of My hands: thy walls are continually before Me" (Isaiah 49:16). Engraving signifies something indelible, inerasable, enduring. How touchingly these engraved stones speak to us of the deep and abiding place believers have in the heart of Christ.

> *"Nothing can the ransomed sever,*
> *Naught divide them from the Lord."*

THE URIM AND THUMMIM

The names, Urim and Thummim, are pure Hebrew words, meaning *Lights* and *Perfection*. For some wise reason the details of how they were placed in the breastplate, and how they worked are not given. Speculation as to this would serve no good purpose. They were put in "the breast plate of judgment", the breastplate evidently acquiring this title because of the Urim and Thummim. Judgment here does not mean condemnation, but discernment and guidance. We speak in everyday speech of a man of sound judgment, that is, of one able to give wise counsel. Psalm 119:66 says, "Teach me good *judgment* and knowledge: for I have believed Thy commandments."

We learn from other Scriptures of its use. For instance, when God was giving instructions to Moses as to his successor, Joshua, He said, "He shall stand before Eleazar the priest, who shall ask counsel for him after the judgment of

Urim before the Lord" (Numbers 27:21). Again we read, "And of Levi He said, Let thy Thummim and thy Urim be with thy Holy One, whom thou didst prove at Massah, and with whom thou didst strive at the waters of Meribah" (Deuteronomy 33:8). Evidently by some means or other in times of stress and national perplexity, enquiries could be made of the Urim and Thummim by the High Priest, and answers given by God Himself.

So we see three things come out clearly in regard to the breastplate:-

1. *The Shoulder Plates spoke of* POWER.
2. *The Breastplate spoke of* LOVE.
3. *The Urim and Thummim spoke of* WISDOM.

This is a perfect combination. We may have love and not power. For instance, a mother has *love*, as she bends in tender solicitude over her dying child, but she has not power to save its life. A rich man may have love and power, and yet lack wisdom, when he gives his loved child every luxury that money can buy, indulging him in every whim and fancy, till for lack of wisdom he has completely ruined the child for life.

But when wisdom, love and power are all united, as they are in the case of our blessed Lord in relation to His people, we have altogether a perfect result. May we rejoice continually in the sense of this.

THE ROBE OF THE EPHOD

The Robe of the Ephod was all of blue, typical of the Heavenly character of our great High Priest. "Seeing then that we have a great High Priest, that is passed into the heavens, Jesus the Son of God, let us hold fast our profession" (Hebrews 4:14). "Christ is not entered into the Holy Places made with hands, which are the figures of the true; but into Heaven itself, now to appear in the presence of God for us" (Hebrews 9:24). How happy we are to be thus represented.

On the hem of this garment were placed pomegranates of blue, and of purple, and of scarlet, and bells of gold, a pomegranate and a bell alternately. The pomegranates spoke of *fruitfulness*, the bells of *testimony*. The colours on the pomegranates spoke of the personal and official glories of the Lord Jesus Christ. The bells of gold spoke of Divine righteousness.

How happy to see that our Lord's fruitfulness (pomegranates) *to* God was equal to His testimony (bells) *for* God. With us things are often unbalanced. Our walk and our talk often do not match. The walk should give power to the talk. The talk should be the product, as it is indeed part, of the walk.

Note in verse 33 of our chapter the pomegranates come first in order, then the bells are mentioned. In the next verse the bell comes first, and then the pomegranate. Why this difference? In life the fruitfulness must be first, before there can be true testimony. Those who testify apart from practising what they teach are like sounding brass and tinkling cymbal.

In the case of our blessed Lord all was perfect and balanced.

In the next verse, as we have said, we find the order reversed. It stands in connection with Aaron going into the Holy Place, and his coming out. When our Lord went into heaven, it was as sounding the glorious news (*bells*) of atonement, completed to God's entire satisfaction, the news of a rent vail, and a glorious resurrection. Then followed the fruits (*pomegranates*), typifying the consequence

of our Lord going in to the presence of God in the outpouring of the Holy Spirit, seen in its blessed
consequences from the wonderful day of Pentecost to this
present time.

THE PLATE OF PURE GOLD ON THE MITRE

This striking ornament had engraven upon it the words
"HOLINESS TO THE LORD", and was bound on a blue lace
on the forefront of the High Priest's Mitre. "And it shall
be upon Aaron's forehead, that Aaron may bear the iniquity of the holy things, which the children of Israel shall
hallow in all their holy gifts: and it shall be always upon
his forehead, that they may be accepted before the LORD"
(verse 38). Everything offered to God must be altogether
holy. But with believers, spite of their assured relationship
before God on the ground of the atoning work of Christ,
there are alas! imperfections and shortcomings. How then
can the believer's offerings to God in worship be accepted?

The golden plate fixed in its prominent place ever testified
in the presence of God to righteousness being fully
accomplished, meeting even the imperfections and shortcomings of the believers' approach to God, taking them
out of the way as before God, so that nothing may be left
but what is of the Holy Spirit of God, even that which is
"HOLINESS TO THE LORD". Blessed and cheering type,
encouraging the believer to come into God's holy presence
with boldness. "Having an High Priest over the house of
God; let us draw near with a true heart in full assurance
of faith, having our hearts sprinkled from an evil conscience, and our bodies washed with pure water"
(Hebrews 10:21-22).

THE EMBROIDERED COAT OF FINE LINEN

This innermost garment speaks of the utter perfection of
the life and walk of our adorable Lord and Saviour. It is

significant that on the Great Day of Atonement the High Priest did not wear his garments of glory and beauty, but this coat of fine linen. Our Lord went to the cross, not in His claims to universal dominion, nor of His kingship over the Jews, but in the perfection of His life, so that death having no claim upon Him, He was able to lay down His life as an atoning sacrifice for sin, and for our eternal blessing.

THE GARMENTS FOR AARON'S SONS

Coats, girdles and bonnets were made for Aaron's sons, and also "linen breeches to cover their nakedness; from the loins even unto the thighs they shall reach" (verse 42). These were put upon Aaron as well as his sons. He could not be a type of Christ in this. Blessed be God, there was no nakedness that needed to be covered in Him. He was absolute perfection. But in the case of Aaron and his sons this careful provision shows that we have to do with a holy God. There must be no presumption in His holy presence.

Chapter 13:
The Consecration of Aaron and His Sons

READ EXODUS 29:1-37

First of all the materials necessary for consecration are enumerated. There were one young bullock, two rams without blemish, unleavened bread, cakes unleavened tempered with oil, and wafers unleavened anointed with oil. All these speak of Christ in one way or another. It is because of what Christ is and what He has done, that the believer is what he is. All depends on Christ.

AARON AND HIS SONS WASHED WITH WATER

What is the significance of being washed by water? As we shall see in a later chapter the priests continually washed their hands and feet at the Brazen Laver, but this was a case of the bath, washing *all over* ceremonially. This was done at their consecration, never to be repeated. Evidently Hebrews 10:22 refers to the consecration of the priests, telling us how the type applies to Christians of this dispensation. "Having our hearts sprinkled from an evil conscience [*typically, the blood of the Sin Offering*], and our bodies washed with pure water [*typically, Aaron and his sons washed all over ceremonially*]."

That both blood and water are cleansing agencies, and both connected with the death of Christ, is evident from John 19:34; "One of the soldiers with a spear pierced His side, and forthwith came there out blood and water." Whilst actual blood and water flowed from the side of the dead Christ, it is evident they have a symbolic meaning, for we read in 1 John 5:6, "This is He that came by water and blood, even Jesus Christ; not by water only, but by water and blood." And again, "There are three that bear witness in earth, the Spirit, and the water, and the blood" (1 John 5:8).

We know that the blood of Christ is for cleansing for we have the Scripture, "The blood of Jesus Christ His Son *cleanseth* us from all sin" (1 John 1:7). To keep things clearly in our minds, we may call this *judicial* cleansing, clearing the believer from the *penalty* of sin once and for all; whereas cleansing by water is for *moral* cleansing, the believer being freed from the *defilement* of sin, and it answers to the new birth by the operation of the Holy Spirit.

The blood is for *judicial* cleansing.
The water is for *moral* cleansing.

The blood cleanses from the *penalty* of sin.
The water cleanses from the *defilement* of sin.

The blood is connected with *righteousness and our standing before God.*
The water is connected with *holiness and state.*

The blood is connected with *Christ's* atoning death alone.
The water is connected with the *Holy Spirit's* operation.

Let these statements be well considered.

Now to prove our statement that water has to do with new birth, without which none of us can enter the kingdom of Heaven, we read, "Except a man be born of water and of the Spirit, he cannot enter into the kingdom of God. That which is born of the flesh is flesh: and that which is born of the Spirit is spirit" (John 3:5-6).

But, says some reader, Does this not mean the rite of baptism? Most assuredly not, and we will give our reasons for this answer. (1) It could not be *Christian* baptism for the simple reason that when our Lord spoke, Christian baptism was not known. The only baptism then was that of John, the Baptist. Christian baptism was not known till *after* Christ had died, for believers are baptized unto the death of Christ. John's baptism was "the baptism of repentance to all the people of Israel" (Acts 13:24). (2) Our Lord spoke of being "*born* of water and of the Spirit". Christian baptism speaks of *death*. "*Buried* with Him by baptism into *death*" (Romans 6:4). *Birth* is life at the beginning of existence; *death* means *burial* at the end of life. Our Lord spoke of being *born* again. He said to Nicodemus, "Ye must be *born again*" (John 3:7). Baptism speaks of *death*. Get it clear in your mind that "being *born* of water and of the Spirit", does not remotely allude to Christian baptism. It is a frightful travesty of the truth to mistake the water of regeneration (*life*) for the water of baptism (*death and burial*). To make out that the rite of baptism makes unconscious infants children of God, and inheritors of the kingdom of God, is a popish figment, designed to put tremendous power into the hands of an arrogant priesthood. Baptism as a *mere* rite never did anything *vital* for anyone. If it did, then all baptized infants would grow up to be true born-again Christians, and alas! we know this is not the case. Infants become Christians, when, coming to years of responsibility, they repent of their sins, and trust the Lord Jesus as their Saviour, and in no other way.

Ephesians 5:25-26 throws great light on the meaning of water as a cleansing agent. We read, "Christ also loved the Church, and gave Himself for it; that He might sanctify it, and cleanse it with *the washing of water* BY THE WORD". Though the simile is changed from "water" to "seed", we find the same thought in connection with 1 Peter 1:23, "Being *born again*, not of corruptible seed, but of incorruptible, BY THE WORD OF GOD". "Of His own will *begat* He us with THE WORD OF TRUTH" (James 1:18). A seed has life in it, and produces life.

But you may ask how can water mean the new birth? Do you not remember the very pregnant statement of our Lord, we have just quoted, "That which is born of the flesh is flesh; and that which is born of the Spirit is spirit" (John 3:6)? This means that the flesh, the evil nature that pertains to all of Adam's race, cannot produce anything but flesh, that which is entirely obnoxious to God. How then can there be anything pleasing to God? There must be a birth of the Holy Spirit, "that which is born of the Spirit is spirit". This means that for moral cleansing there must be a new nature. Think this over, and you will be convinced of the truth of it.

An illustration may help. A traveller in Italy got belated one evening, and had to find a lodging for the night up among the mountains. He got accommodation in a humble cottage. The room assigned to him had a very filthy floor. The traveller was about to ask the woman of the house to clean the floor, when he noticed it was a mud floor. Hot water, soap and scrubbing applied to the mud floor would only have made more mud. "That which is born of the flesh is flesh". You cannot alter the nature of anything by outside means.

What then was the alternative? How could the traveller get a clean floor? The only way to accomplish this would be to get a NEW floor, made of materials capable of being kept clean. So the flesh cannot be improved, not even in Nicodemus, a ruler of the Jews. A NEW floor is necessary, in other words a NEW *life* is necessary, and that is brought about by the word of God acting on the individual in the power of the Spirit of God, producing NEW *birth*. "BORN of water and of the Spirit", predicates a NEW *life* by the agency of water (the word of God) and the power of the Holy Spirit.

Augustus Toplady wrote long ago:

> *"Rock of Ages, cleft for me,*
> *Let me hide myself in Thee,*
> *Let the WATER and the BLOOD*
> *From Thy riven side which flowed*
> *Be of sin the DOUBLE cure,*
> *Cleanse me from its GUILT and POWER."*

Evidently the poet had grasped the meaning of *judicial* cleansing by blood, and *moral* cleansing by the impartation of a new life.

There is a well-known Scripture, which clearly shows the difference of the bath, being washed *all over*, and the *daily* washing of hands and feet, as the priests did at the Brazen Laver. Our Lord in washing the feet of His disciples as a symbolic act, said, "He that is washed [Greek, *louo, to wash the* WHOLE *body*] needeth not save to wash [Greek, *nipto, to wash* A PART *of the body*] his feet, but is clean every whit" (John 13:10). The first washing answers to the ceremonial washing of the priests *all over*, never to be repeated; the second, to the washing of the hands and feet in the Brazen Laver *repeatedly*.

It is interesting and helpful to see how truths dovetail in such an exact way in Scripture. When we remember that the writers were separated by centuries from each other, and that the earlier writers could not know what the later writers would say, it is a wonderful mark of inspiration to see this, and how there is only one Mind behind the whole Bible, the mind of God. We see blood and water flowing from the side of a dead Christ, and that sets forth that which is the fountain spring of everything. We find blood and water in the Tabernacle, blood upon the Mercy Seat, water in the Brazen Laver. We find water and blood in the consecration of Aaron and his sons; water, the washing all over; blood, the Sin Offering necessary for their approach to God. We find water necessary for new birth in John 3, and in the same chapter the necessity that the Son of Man should be lifted up on the cross, must die, must shed His precious blood. In John 13:10, we have seen how there are two Greek words for wash, one to wash *all over*, the other to wash *a part*, answering to the washing all over of the priests on the day of their consecration, and then washing a part answering to the Brazen Laver. Finally we saw in Hebrews 10:22, "Our hearts sprinkled from an evil conscience [*the blood*], and our bodies washed with pure water." We find Scripture giving clear testimony as to this.

The washing ceremonially of Aaron and his sons brings out the truth of the vital necessity for all, who approach God, of being born again, having a nature suitable to Him and His holiness. We can sum up the matter. There are two grand results of the death of Christ, one to do with man's guilt (the blood); the other to do with his state (Divine life). We read, "In this was manifested the love of God toward us, because that God sent His only begotten Son into the world, that we might live [*involving the impartation of the Divine life in the New Birth*] through Him. Herein is love, not that we loved God, but that He loved us, and sent His Son to be the propitiation [*cleansing by blood*] for our sins" (1 John 4:9-10).

Aaron Clothed and Anointed

Aaron is first clothed in the garments of glory and beauty, surely typical of Christ as Representative of His people, in their relation as priests to Him, who is the High Priest. The anointing oil was poured upon His head, typical of Christ "having received of the Father the promise of the Holy Ghost" (Acts 2:33), and thus taking up His office before God.

Then Aaron's sons were clothed with linen coats, girdles and bonnets, thus set in relation to Aaron as the High Priest, typical of how all believers to-day are priests in relation to Christ the High Priest.

The Sin Offering

A bullock was then brought to the Door of the Tabernacle of the Congregation. Aaron and his sons put their hands on the head of the bullock. This was symbolic of their accepting the sacrifice as necessary for the question of meeting their guilt. All the sinfulness of Aaron and his sons was thereby in figure transferred to the sacrifice. The bullock was then slain. They would mark its death as the fatal blow fell upon it. They would see its quivering death agonies, and learn therein feebly, and in picture, what a serious thing sin is, and how only death can meet it. Part of the blood was put upon the horns of the Altar, and the rest poured out at the bottom of the Altar. The life is in the blood, and this act testifies that death alone can meet the penalty of sin, only death and that an atoning death, and none could furnish that but the Son of God.

The fat parts of the bullock, viz. the fat covering the inwards, the caul above the liver, the two kidneys, and the fat upon them, were burned upon the Altar of Burnt Offering. These went up as "a sweet savour unto the Lord", for nothing was burned upon the Brazen Altar, but what went up as entirely acceptable unto the Lord.

The fat parts being burned upon the Altar typified, that, even in this most serious type of the death of Christ, there was in the most inward springs of Christ's devotedness to the will of God, that which was most delightful to the heart of God. Indeed the burning of the fat parts comes first, as if this aspect of Christ's death is ever before God. Never could this have been manifested in its fullness and depth as at the cross of Calvary.

The rest of the bullock—his flesh, his skin, his dung—was burned outside the camp. It was a Sin Offering, which was always burned outside the camp. Outside the camp was a place of reproach. We read, "The bodies of those beasts, whose blood is brought into the Sanctuary by the High Priest for sin, are burned *without the camp.* Wherefore Jesus also, that He might sanctify the people with His own blood, suffered *without the gate*" (Hebrews 13:11-12). The camp was a large place. Some three million souls surrounded the Tabernacle. According to the Jewish historian, the camp had a circuit of twelve miles. It must have been a solemn and awe-inspiring spectacle to see the Sin Offering being carried outside the camp, there to be burned as symbolizing God's utter detestation of sin, and the death of our Lord as alone meeting the judgment of God.

> *"There is a green hill far away*
> *Without a city wall,*
> *Where the dear Lord was crucified,*
> *Who died to save us all."*

The flesh of the Sin Offering was burned, setting forth that which is general. The flesh is altogether bad. The dung too was burned. The dung, the excreta of the animal, represents what is recognized as bad even among men, the excesses of sin, such as drunkenness, dishonesty, blasphemy, uncleanness and the like. All can understand the dung being burned.

But the skin, the beauty of the animal, was likewise burned. Here we have a very different lesson. Not only does man's worst come under God's judgment at the cross, but his best. This is a hard lesson to learn, but a very necessary one.

Job, as it were, had a handsome skin. Honest, upright, benevolent, generous, kind-hearted, yet he had to learn that his best was but vileness in God's sight. To his three friends he stoutly maintained his own righteousness. But when he found himself in God's presence, he exclaimed, "I have heard of Thee by the hearing of the ear; but now mine eye seeth Thee. Wherefore I abhor myself, and repent in dust and ashes" (Job 42:5-6). The skin of the bullock was burned.

Saul of Tarsus had a handsome skin metaphorically. He could boast, "If any other man thinketh that he hath whereof he might trust in the flesh, I more ... concerning ... righteousness, which is in the law [I *was*] blameless" (Philippians 3:4-6). In the light of that which was above the brightness of the sun he learned the humbling truth as to himself. The proud Pharisee was brought to confess what he truly was in God's holy presence. He wrote, "This is a faithful saying, and worthy of all acceptation, that Christ Jesus came into the world to save sinners; of whom I AM CHIEF" (1 Timothy 1:15). In him God showed forth

His whole longsuffering. The skin of the bullock was burned.

It is well to learn the lesson of the skin being burned as well as the dung. The best the flesh can offer to God is no more acceptable than the worst. "That which is highly esteemed among men is abomination in the sight of God" (Luke 16:15), is a hard lesson to learn.

In connection with the sacrifices, it is noticeable that there are two words in the Hebrew language for burning. The word used in connection with the Brazen Altar for. burning is *gatar*, a word used for the burning of incense, that which is a sweet-smelling odour, rising UP *to God* to His delight. The word used in connection with the Sin Offering burned outside the camp is *saraph*, which means to consume with intense heat. It is a word of dire significance, speaking only of condign [10] punishment, a terrible word, signifying the wrath of a thrice-holy God, *coming* DOWN i*n unsparing judgment*. God would teach us by this latter word the awful heinousness of sin, and thus the meaning of Calvary.

On similar lines it is a striking fact that there is only one word in the Hebrew (*chattath*) for sin and Sin Offering. So we read of our Lord being so identified with the sins He atoned for on the cross, that it could be said, "He hath made Him to be sin for us, who knew no sin; that we might be made the righteousness of God in Him" (2 Corinthians 5:21). Could the awful meaning of the cross be more powerfully portrayed than by the fact that our Lord, who knew no sin, was made the sin He abhorred, as He only could abhor it? Surely the believer is bound by the tenderest ties of Divine love to our Lord, who entered upon such a path, and did such a work at such a cost to Himself. Words entirely fail us here.

THE TWO RAMS AND THEIR TYPICAL MEANING

Two rams were sacrificed in connection with the consecration of Aaron and his sons. The first ram was a Burnt Offering. The second was "a Ram of Consecration".

Aaron and his sons put their hands on the head of the first ram. It was slain, its blood sprinkled round about the Altar, cut in pieces, and the whole burned upon the Altar, as a Burnt Offering.

This presents us with an aspect of the death of Christ different from the Sin Offering which we have just considered. The distinction between the two should be grasped.

The Sin Offering spoke of God's unsparing judgment upon sin. The judgment *comes* DOWN upon the sacrifice.

The Burnt Offering emphasized Christ's devotedness to the will of God, leading Him to lay down His life at the cross as an atonement for sin. The sweet savour of the burning *goes* UP as incense to God.

In the Sin Offering all the *demerit* of the offerer in the laying on of hands was transferred typically to the offering, and the offering was charged with all the guilt of the offerer. "Who His own self bare our sins in His own body on the tree" (1 Peter 2:24).

In the Burnt Offering all the *merit* of the sacrifice was transferred in the laying on of hands to the offerer, who thereby stood in all the acceptance of the offering. "Accepted in the Beloved" (Ephesians 1:6). If never a sinner were blest through it, that offering of Christ through the eternal Spirit would still be altogether pleasing to God. The laying on of hands speaks of full and complete *identification*.

"A Ram of Consecration"

Aaron and his sons put their hands on the head of "the other ram". It was slain, and the blood put "upon the tip of the right ear of Aaron, and upon the tip of the right ear of his sons, and upon the thumb of their right hand, and upon the great toe of their right foot" (Exodus 29:20).

This second ram was called "a ram of consecration". By this significant ritual we learn in type that God calls upon believers to be consecrated to Him. He claims their ears, that they receive His communications and instructions. He claims their hands for willing service to Him. He claims their feet, that their walk before Him should be fully to Him. Our lives were forfeited because of sin, and we receive life and pardon through the death of our Lord, and this gives God a claim in full measure upon all that we are and have.

> *"Were the whole realm of nature mine,*
> *That were an offering far too small;*
> *Love so amazing, so Divine,*
> *Demands my soul, my life, my all."*

"The love of Christ constraineth us; because we thus judge, that if one died for all, then were all dead: and that He died for all, that they which live should not henceforth live unto themselves, but UNTO HIM, which died for them and rose again" (2 Corinthians 5:14-15).

The Sprinkling with Blood and Oil

Moses was then instructed to take of the Blood that was upon the Altar, and of the Anointing Oil, and sprinkle Aaron and his sons, and their garments, therewith. Thus were the priests and their garments hallowed.

It is by the efficacy of Christ's atoning death (*blood*), and the action of the Holy Spirit (*oil*) that believers are constituted priests. The believer is thus brought into association with Christ, who has won by His death our place of nearness and approach to God, the Holy Spirit being the power whereby we appropriate this favoured place. From the One, who died at Calvary, was given the Holy Spirit from Heaven to link believers up with Himself in glory.

THE WAVE AND HEAVE OFFERINGS

The fat parts of the Ram of Consecration were taken by Moses with the right shoulder, a loaf of bread, a cake of oiled bread, and one wafer of unleavened bread, and put into the hands of Aaron and his sons, and they were to wave them before the LORD. Moses was then to burn them upon the Altar as a Burnt Offering, a sweet savour before the LORD. The Hebrew words for consecration, *mala yad*, mean *to fill the hands*.

What answers to this in Christianity is the heart filled with Christ, the overflowing of a heart occupied with Christ, rising up to God in worship. The fat parts of the ram speak of the strength of our Lord's devotedness to the will of His Father, even unto death.

The right shoulder only strengthens the idea of our Lord's devotedness to the will of God, even to death. The shoulder is emblematic of strength. The loaf of bread speaks generally of the perfection of our Lord's life. The cake of oiled bread sets forth that just as the cake was permeated with oil, so "God giveth not the Spirit by measure unto Him" (John 3:34). Our Lord was filled with the Holy Spirit of God from His birth as a Man in this world. The one wafer was evidently anointed with oil, for in other Scriptures it is so, and would typify how our Lord was anointed for service at His baptism, the Holy Spirit descending like a dove upon Him. The right shoulder would point to the atoning sacrifice of the cross, all that

He was in life contributing to what He was in death, the perfect willing Sacrifice, bringing such glory to God and blessing to us.

We have seen how the *right shoulder* was waved before the LORD, now we find the *breast* of the wave offering united with the shoulder of the heave offering being sanctified as the portion for Aaron and his sons to eat. This stands for the believer entering into the strength (*shoulder*) and efficacy of the atoning death of Christ, and the Divine affection (*breast*) of the Lord that carried Him through the dread ordeal of the cross.

The wave and heave offerings took the character of peace or communion offerings. How sweet it is for saints to have thoughts in common with God about Christ, and to feed upon the wondrous thoughts of His love, which spring from the sacrifice of Himself.

Aaron and his sons were to seethe the flesh of the Ram of consecration in the Holy Place, and eat of it with the bread of consecration. Two provisos were made.

1.   *Only the consecrated priests were to eat of it.*

2.   *They had to eat it on one day, nothing was to remain over to the next day.*

This teaches us that only believers are entitled to be in God's presence as worshippers, and that it must be in the power of *present* communion that these wondrous spiritual things can be enjoyed.

Finally the ceremony of consecration was to be repeated, and the Altar cleansed, daily for seven days, indicating the perfection (*seven*) that must ever mark that with which God has to do. Surely the priests would never forget the lessons of sacrifice and holiness all their earthly days. May we Christians learn these lessons more and more deeply as we enter into the truth of them.

Chapter 14:
The Golden Altar of Incense and the Brazen Laver

READ EXODUS 30:1-10, 17-21

The description of the Golden Altar of incense and the Brazen Laver is designedly left, as we have already seen, till the priests were consecrated, whose privilege it was to use them, for they had to do with the work of the priests, and their entering in to the service of the Sanctuary.

We have seen how God *comes* OUT in Christ as the Apostle of our profession. We are now about to see how Christ has *gone* IN as the High Priest of our profession, leading His own into the very presence of God for worship.

The *pure gold,* as seen in the Golden Altar, comes before the *brass* as seen in the Laver. The Altar comes before the Laver, the inside before the outside, which is ever God's way. The reason is obvious.

The Golden Altar gives us the *place* of the worshipper.

The Brazen Laver gives us the *condition* of the worshipper.

The place comes before the condition, because the place is won for us by what comes out at the Brazen Altar, and the meaning of the blood upon the Mercy Seat, even by the atoning death of our Lord Jesus Christ. Righteousness (*blood*) has won the *place* for us; holiness (*water*) is the necessary *condition* for the enjoyment of that place. Hence the Laver. Let us never confound place and condition. To do so is to cloud the soul, for it is the fruitful source of doubts and fears.

THE GOLDEN ALTAR OF INCENSE

The materials of which this article was made, viz. Shittim wood overlaid with pure gold, speak as before of the true Manhood and supreme Deity of our Lord Jesus Christ. The rings and staves remind us that we are still in the wilderness, and have not yet reached the Heavenly Canaan.

Its position was "before the vail that is by the Ark of the Testimony, before the Mercy Seat that is over the Testimony, where I will meet with thee" (Exodus 30:6). The vail is still up in the type, in the antitype the vail is rent, there is now only one Holy Place—all has now the character of the Holiest of All.

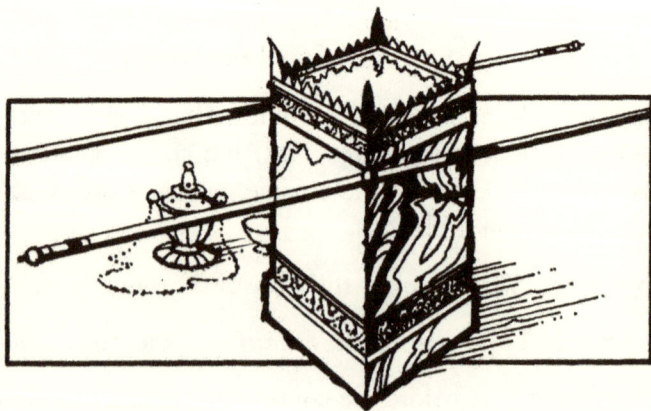

On the Golden Altar Aaron had to burn incense every morning and evening, typical of our High Priest's intercession, presenting the fragrance of what Christ is and what He has done as upholding His people in the presence of God. So we read, "Having therefore, brethren, boldness to enter into the Holiest by the blood of Jesus … *and having an High Priest over the house of God*; let us draw near … in full assurance of faith" (Hebrews 10:19-22).

Further, no strange incense was to be offered on the Golden Altar. None but the High Priest was qualified to offer incense at that Altar. Nadab and Abihu, the sons of Aaron, took their censers, putting fire and incense therein, and offering strange fire before the LORD, contrary to the commandment, and paid the penalty with their lives. "And there went out fire from the LORD, and devoured them, and they died before the LORD" (Leviticus 10:2). Only believers in communion have the right to enter the presence of the Lord, and that because of the intercession of our Lord on their behalf, supporting them in that wonderful place, the very presence of God. No burnt sacrifice, no meat offering, no drink offerings were to take place at the Golden Altar of incense. These were dealt with at the Brazen Altar, the place of atonement, whereas the Golden Altar of incense was the place for the worshipper, as maintained there by the intercession of our Lord Jesus.

There is a peculiar word used here for "burn" [Hebrew, *Alah*] only twice used in Scripture, and that in connection with the lamps burning before the Golden Altar of incense. It carries the significance of *causing to go* UP.

THE BRAZEN LAVER

The Laver was made of brass, and contained water only, where the priests could cleanse their hands and feet from defilement before going into the presence of God in the Sanctuary.

There was no measurement given for the Laver, for there is no limit to the holiness that God would wish His people to show. "Be ye holy: for I am holy" (1 Peter 1:16) is the standard given by God.

The priests, bathed all over ceremonially, were to keep up cleanliness practically and daily. The Laver was provided for that purpose.

The washing of hands and feet in the Brazen Laver sets forth that for the defilement, which is contracted in passing through this evil world, cleansing is necessary. It is not a question of actual sin, which is a grave matter, needing the office of our Lord as our Advocate with the Father. For instance a believer might be employed in a place where loose talk and swearing were indulged in, which could easily fix itself on his memory, though refused by him in his spirit. He goes to a meeting, and in that atmosphere, or by private meditation, his memory is freed from occupation with these defiling things, and the believer is set free in spirit to be occupied with the Lord's things. This is what is typified in the Brazen Laver. Or a Christian's mind might be burdened with business things, quite legitimate in their place. He would have need to have his feet washed, that ministry from our Lord, or through one of His own, would free his mind to be occupied with the Lord's things. Remember the washing is by *water*, setting forth that it is connected with *moral* condition of soul before the Lord.

In the Old Testament the hands and feet were washed; in the New Testament the feet only. Why this difference? The answer is simple. The hands of the Jewish priests had to do with gory sacrifices, and would therefore get defiled; the feet got defiled in the dust and stain of the desert and of the camp. Thank God, there is no need in Christianity for what answers to the hands being washed, for the Sacrifice of our Lord is completed, and the believer stands in the presence of God without a stain. In Judaism the sacrifices were repeated again and again, for the blood of bulls and goats could never take away sin,

> *"But Christ, the spotless Lamb,*
> *Took all our guilt away,*
> *A Sacrifice of nobler name,*
> *And richer blood than they."*

The defiling influence of the world is all around us, even when most sheltered from it. The need of the spiritual cleansing of the spirit, symbolized by the feet washing, remains. For this we have the blessed ministry of the Lord, so that we may have "part with Him". Our Lord in this has graciously given us an example. If our Lord and Master has washed our feet, we also ought to wash one another's feet.

THE WOMEN'S BRAZEN LOOKING GLASSES

It is said of Bezaleel that "he made the Laver of Brass, and the foot of it of brass, of the looking-glasses [AV margin, *brasen glasses*] of the women assembling, which assembled at the Door of the Tabernacle of the Congregation" (Exodus 38:8). The brazen mirrors, which had oftentimes been the instruments of self-gratification, for the display of that which springs from the flesh, were surrendered to the service of the LORD, and employed in that which typified the need of personal holiness. "Follow ... holiness, without which no man shall see the Lord" (Hebrews 12:14). Do we as Christians surrender everything that would give us status in this world, so as to be free in spirit for God's presence and service?

"THE SEA OF GLASS"

It is interesting to see the end of God's ways on this line. The Brazen Laver of the wilderness gave place to the "Molten Sea of the Temple". Standing on twelve molten oxen with five Lavers on the right hand and five on the left, it must have been a wonderful sight. The priests used the lavers for the washing of the Burnt Offering, "but the sea was for the priests to wash in" (2 Chronicles 4:6). At last when the Church is raptured to glory, and the Lord's people are beyond the reach of defilement, we have the sea of glass. "And I saw as it were *a sea of glass* mingled with fire: and them that had gotten the victory over the Beast, and over his image, and over his mark, and over the number of his name, *stand on the sea of glass*, having the harps of God. And they SING," etc. (Revelation 15:2-3). No longer do they *wash* in the Laver, no longer is there the need of feet washing, no longer are they in a defiling scene, but standing on a sea of glass, symbolic of a state of fixed and absolute holiness in a scene where naught that defiles shall ever enter, they stand and SING in holy exultation the Song of Moses and the Song of the Lamb. All that hinders communion and joy for ever left behind. Nothing but bliss and joy unspeakable left.

It is very significant that between the description of the Golden Altar and that of the Brazen Laver, there is interposed instruction as to the numbering of the children of Israel, and the necessity of the atonement money as the only ground on which typically God could have to do with sinful people, thus emphasizing that the foundation of all our blessing lies in the atoning sacrifice of our Lord Jesus Christ.

Chapter 15:
The Offerings

READ LEVITICUS 1 TO 7

In writing of the Offerings it would be well to make a few prefatory remarks. A good general survey always helps to an intelligent grasp of the details.

The principal Offerings were five in number.

1. *The Burnt Offering.*
2. *The Meat Offering.*
3. *The Peace Offering.*
4. *The Sin Offering.*
5. *The Trespass Offering.*

These in their turn were divided into three and two.

The Sweet Savour Offerings were burned upon the Brazen Altar. The first three of our list belonged to that category.

The Sin Offerings were burned "outside the camp". The last two of our list belong to this category.

The Sweet Savour Offerings spoke of God's delight in our Lord's surrender to His will in making atonement on the cross.

The Sin Offerings spoke of the fierce judgment of God upon sin when the load of our sins was laid on the Holy Sufferer.

The following will give at a glance the things offered, and show to the careful observer somewhat of their differences and detail.

THE BURNT OFFERING

Bullock, a male without blemish.

Ram, a male of sheep or goats without blemish.

Fowls, turtle doves or young pigeons.

THE MEAT OFFERING

Flour, oil, frankincense, unleavened cakes mingled with oil. Fine flour with oil, green ears dried by the fire, oil and frankincense thereon.

THE PEACE OFFERING

Of the herd, male or female.

Of the flock, male or female.

THE SIN OFFERING

FOR THE ANOINTED PRIEST—
Young bullock without blemish.

FOR THE WHOLE CONGREGATION—
A [young] bullock without blemish.

FOR A RULER—
Kid of the goats, male without blemish.

FOR ONE OF THE COMMON PEOPLE—
Kid of the goats, female without blemish.

Lamb, female without blemish.

The Trespass Offering

Female lamb, or kid.

Two *turtle doves* or two *young pigeons*.

Tenth part of an ephah of *flour*.

In the holy things of the Lord—

Ram, without blemish, restitution, and fifth part added.

A trespass against the Lord—

Ram, without blemish, restitution, and fifth part added.

It will be noticed that a bullock is a higher class of sacrifice than a *young* bullock; that a male is higher than a female; and that the lowest type of sacrifice were the turtle doves, or young pigeons or even fine flour. It can be seen at a glance that the higher the sinner was, the greater his privileges before God, the greater his sin in the sight of God. This is on the lines that "unto whomsoever much is given, of him shall be much required" (Luke 12:48).

It will be seen there is a distinct order. God begins at the Burnt Offering, the highest type of Offering. The sinner in his experience begins with the Trespass Offering. Just as God began with the Ark, and the Holiest of All, as we have already seen, began as it were at the very top with His own glory, rather than with the sinner's need, though His glory includes meeting the sinner's need, so here God begins with the Burnt Offering, the highest aspect of the death of Christ, an *atoning* death even in this aspect.

Just as the prism splits light into its seven amazing colours, the blending of which gives perfection, viz. pure light, so the death of Christ in its varied aspects, grouped together in our mind, helps to a fuller and richer understanding of the death of Christ.

The Bible gives no quarter to Unitarianism, Higher Criticism and Modernism with their denial of what is fundamental to Christianity. Sacrifice, blood-shedding, death of victim, burning, ashes—all emphasize with a mighty voice that the death of Christ was sacrificial, vicarious, atoning. To rob it of these meanings or weaken them is to make the death of Christ perfectly meaningless. To present Christ's death as that only of a martyr, or as an inspiring example to mankind, is to mock a sin-stricken, death-marked race with a crueller deception than the mocking mirage of the desert, deceiving the traveller dying of thirst, leading its already exhausted victim to a last despairing effort, only ending in death. To pretend that the sacrificial aspect of the death of Christ is not in the Scriptures, is to call black white, and white black, deceiving none but the willingly ignorant.

Chapter 16:
The Burnt Offering

READ LEVITICUS 1

This is the Offering, which presents the death of Christ in its highest aspect. The Hebrew word, *Olah*, translated Burnt Offering, means *"that which goes up"*, that which ascends. It was a *voluntary* Offering, presenting Christ typically as the One who voluntarily offered Himself to God, even as an atoning sacrifice for sin. It should be carefully noted that ATONEMENT is connected with it. It was burnt upon the Brazen Altar, and gives the Altar the name of "The Altar of Burnt Offering" (Exodus 30:28; 40:10). We read, "In burnt offerings and sacrifices for sin Thou hast had no pleasure. Then said I, Lo, I come (in the volume of the book it is written of Me), to do Thy will, O God" (Hebrews 10:6-7). That will took Him to the cross, for the settlement of sin, securing God's glory in fullest measure.

THE LAYING ON OF HANDS

The laying on of hands denoted identification of the offerer with the offering. He was met by the words, "It shall be accepted for him to make atonement for him." The laying on of hands in this case was very significant. It meant all the *merit* of the Sacrifice was transferred in type to the offerer, so that he stood in all the acceptance of the offering at the hands of God. The offerer was thus brought into Divine favour.

Christ's death in this aspect was alluded to by the Apostle Paul in writing, "To the praise of the glory of His grace, wherein He hath made us *accepted* IN THE BELOVED" (Ephesians 1:6). The Beloved is Christ, but we do well to meditate on the reason why the word, "Beloved", is chosen. It is the only time our Lord is so designated. If the Scripture had said that we were accepted in Christ, that would have been true but hardly sufficient, for the Spirit of God would emphasize the warmth and wonderful nature of the acceptance in which our blessed Lord stands before God as our Representative. So the Spirit of God uses the endearing word, "BELOVED". We can sing with joy,

"So dear, so very dear to God,
We cannot dearer be;
For in the person of the Son,
We are as dear as He."

In this aspect of Christ's death we learn how wonderfully acceptable and fragrant was the atoning death of our Lord to the One who sent Him. All that was burned on the Burnt Offering Altar went up as "a sweet savour to God".

DIFFERENT VALUES IN THE ANIMALS SACRIFICED

1. *Of the herd, a bullock without blemish.*
2. *Of the flock, a sheep or goat without blemish.*
3. *Of fowls, turtle doves or young pigeons.*

The bullock is more valuable than a sheep or goat; the sheep or goat more valuable than the turtle doves or young pigeons. This presents to us the varying degrees of appreciation the believer has of the death of Christ. But, thank God, the sacrifice of pigeons was accepted equally with that of a bullock. We are accepted, not according to the measure of our apprehension of the death of Christ, but of God's full and perfect appreciation of the death of Christ. None of us can rise to this height, but God accepts us on the ground of what *He* thinks of the death of His Son. This is a source of great comfort to us, and would give us confidence to praise God for His unspeakable gift.

The bullock without blemish was the highest form of sacrifice. On the part of the offerer it typifies a very high appreciation of the death of Christ. The offerer was to slay the bullock. The priest then sprinkled the blood about the Altar. Nothing short of blood-shedding can make atonement for sin. The Burnt Offering was then flayed, and cut into his pieces, typifying God's appreciation *in detail* of all that led Christ to offer up His life on the cross. Fire was placed upon the Altar, and wood laid in order thereon.

Then the priests were to lay the parts—the head and fat—upon the Altar, the inward parts were to be washed in water, and all was consumed upon the Altar. The inwards and legs washed in water typify Christ in the inward springs of His being (*the inwards*), and in all the detail and energy of His walk (*the legs*). It has been well said by another [J. N. Darby], "As to the washing with water, it made the sacrifice typically what Christ was *essentially*—pure." All was to be burnt on the Altar.

The key to the understanding of this beautiful type of the death of Christ lies in two main ideas. First, the word for *burning* typifies the ascending in fragrance up to God of the wonderful devotion of our Lord in giving Himself to death in carrying out the will of God. It is a word that is used for the burning of incense, fragrance ascending.

Second, it carried with it the thought of the *acceptance* of the offerer. If there never had been a sinner saved through the atoning death of our Lord, yet His death would have glorified God as nothing else could have done. Christ's devotedness to the will of God in this was delightful to the heart of God.

The offering of a sheep or goat "without blemish" suggests a less vivid appreciation of the death of Christ, but yet most precious and acceptable to God, precious as *He* knows so fully the value of that perfect offering of our Lord upon the cross. But being a Burnt Offering, the animal sacrificed had to be a *male*, typical of the dignity and blessedness of this presentation of the work of Christ.

But an offerer might be poor. The bullock, or even the sheep or goat, might be quite beyond his means. Provision was made for such. He was allowed to bring turtle doves or young pigeons. Grace would meet and appreciate the feeblest apprehension of the death of Christ, which would not abate one iota of the acceptance wherewith the offerer was accepted, for that depended, not on the offerer's apprehension, but on the value GOD sets on that wondrous sacrifice.

The crop and feathers of the birds were cast away, typifying that the worshipper may mix up unworthy and unacceptable thoughts of Christ's death with what is worthy and acceptable. In the case of the bullock, or the sheep or goat, all was burned upon the Altar, but in this case the crop and feathers were cast by the east side of the Altar by the place of the ashes, showing that unworthy thoughts of Christ must perish.

The birds were cleft in two, but short of being wholly severed asunder, again typifying poverty of apprehension, as if the worshipper could travel thus far on the right road, but had not the strength of apprehension to go the whole way.

And yet how touching is the grace of God in meeting such a case. How cheering to such to be greeted by the same words as were given to the offerer of the bullock or sheep or goat, "It is a burnt sacrifice, an offering made by fire, of a sweet savour unto the LORD."

The head was to be burned upon the Altar, while the blood was wrung out at the side of the Altar. Nothing short of blood would meet the case. Poorly as we have presented this wonderful sacrifice, it may encourage us to desire enlargement of soul in the apprehension of this wondrous aspect of the death of Christ.

Chapter 17:
The Meat Offering

READ LEVITICUS 2

The Hebrew word used in this case is *Minchah*, simply meaning an offering, a word always employed for the Meat Offering. The materials of which this offering was composed was never "meat", as we speak of the flesh of animals. It was always composed of things baked in the oven, such as cakes and wafers, and sometimes of green ears of corn.

This Offering presents to us the beautiful humanity of our Lord, so delightful to the Father, that the heavens could be opened upon Him, and attention drawn to Him as the One in whom God was well pleased. Though our Lord was a perfect Man of God's delight and pleasure on this earth, yet we must never forget He was "God blessed for ever" (Romans 9:5).

Seeing there is no blood-shedding connected with this sacrifice, it clearly presents the death of Christ as the culmination of a life lived upon earth that was fully to God's glory, the whole headed up, as it were, in His death. The Meat Offering, therefore, presents typically the death of Christ, not as in its atoning efficacy, but on the lines of

Philippians 2:5-11, where we are exhorted to have the same mind as Christ Jesus, who being on equality with God, for He was God, stooped down to man's estate, took upon Himself the form of a servant, and became obedient to death even the death of the cross. Our Lord's death gathered up all that He was in life, and the whole was presented to God for His delight and ours.

The Meat Offering was to be of fine flour without leaven and oil poured upon it. The fine flour typified the beautiful life of our Lord. Just as flour is smooth and without grit, so our Lord's life was perfect in every detail. Oil poured upon it sets forth that the Lord, as a dependent Man on earth, received the Holy Spirit in fullest measure. Frankincense poured upon it tells us that that wonderful life was ever fragrant to God. Every word, every footfall of His, was as sweetest music in the ear of God.

A handful of this fine flour, with oil and frankincense put upon it, was burned by the priest upon the Altar as a memorial, "an offering made by fire, of a sweet savour unto the LORD." There is no separating Christ's life from His death. We, Christians, could not in any way touch His life, save as His death has met our sins, as will be seen in the Sin Offering, and given us acceptance, as we have seen in the Burnt Offering.

The remnant of the Meat Offering belonged to Aaron and his sons, beautiful reminder that God gives His people to enjoy that which delights His own heart.

The Meat Offering could be treated in three ways,

1. *Baken in the oven.*
2. *Baken in a pan.*
3. *Baken in a frying pan.*

These seem to indicate the different intensities of trials and sufferings by which Christ was tested in life and death, and in all of which He was perfect. *The oven* speaks of that which is out of sight, and may typify the hidden out-of-sight sufferings of mind and spirit that the Lord passed through, known only to His Father. We read of our Lord "groaning in Himself" at the grave of Lazarus. None of us with senses blunted by sin can ever realize what suffering our Lord went through in spirit as He met sorrow and sin in this world. He was indeed "a Man of sorrows and acquainted with grief" (Isaiah 53:3).

The pan may speak of the more public sufferings of our Lord in this world. He told His disciples, how He must "suffer many things of the elders, and chief priests and scribes" (Matthew 16:21). We have only to read the four Gospels to see what our Lord suffered in His path of testimony.

The frying pan may speak of that which is still more intensive, and include even the cross itself. In everything the Lord was perfect. Is it the temptation in the wilderness for forty days, when the Devil presented a threefold enticement, which with us would have appealed to the lust of the flesh, the lust of the eyes, the pride of life? He came out unscathed, untouched by breath of evil, unmarked by touch of failure. Is it the want of that understanding and sympathy which His disciples should have shown? Is it in all the sore trials He endured that marked His path; nay, was it in the cross itself with its fiery trial? In everything He was absolutely perfect.

The details given bring out these thoughts clearly. They speak of

1. *Unleavened cakes of fine flour mingled with oil.*
2. *Unleavened wafers anointed with oil.*

In both cases the Offering was to be *unleavened*, no evil in our Lord's life answered to this. In both cases it had to be of fine flour, again emphasizing the absolute perfection of His life.

"Mingled with oil", what can be the meaning of this? It sets forth that our Lord in His human nature was filled with the Holy Spirit of God. Oil is typical of the Holy Spirit. Our Lord was begotten by the Holy Spirit of the Virgin Mary. From His birth it could be said, "God giveth not the Spirit by measure unto Him" (John 3:34).

Anointed with oil is typical of the day when our Lord was baptized, and stepped into public service for God and man. "And, lo! the heavens were opened unto Him, and He saw the Spirit of God descending like a dove, and lighting upon Him" (Matthew 3:16). The Hebrew word *Messiah*, and its Greek equivalent *Christ*, means the Anointed One. "God anointed Jesus of Nazareth with the Holy Ghost and with power; who went about doing good, and healing all that were oppressed of the devil; for God was with Him" (Acts 10:38).

There were two things that were forbidden in the Offerings of the LORD made by fire, viz. leaven and honey. *Leaven* typifies evil. To mix up the holy things of the Lord and evil is abomination to God. This was seen in the case of Eli's sons, Hophni and Phinehas. These two men were "priests of the LORD", that was their office, and yet in their practice they were described, "The sons of Eli were sons of Belial; they knew not the LORD" (1 Samuel 2:12). There followed a most tragic breakdown in the history of Israel. Eli fell dead, his two sons killed in battle, and the Ark of the LORD taken by the Philistines.

Honey typifies that which is pleasant to nature, such as natural affection, links of friendship, and the like. Nature has its place, but not in the things of the Lord. To be "without natural affection" (2 Timothy 3:3) is a sign of the last and perilous times. When the relationships of life are flouted, and men and women live only to gratify their selfish desires and lusts, surely the last days have arrived.

But when it comes to the things of the Lord, Scripture announces a great truth, "Henceforth know we no man after the flesh: yea, though we have known Christ after the flesh, yet now henceforth know we Him no more" (2 Corinthians 5:16).

A Scriptural illustration comes to hand. When Moses cried for volunteers to avenge the dishonour put upon the Lord's name in the matter of the worship of the golden calf, the sons of Levi responded. Moses said, "Thus saith the LORD God of Israel, put every man his sword by his side, and go in and out from gate to gate throughout the camp, and slay every man *his brother*, and every man *his companion*, and every man *his neighbour*" (Exodus 32:27). Here we have an example where the claims of the LORD stood before the claims of nature. Honey had not to assert itself at a time of stress in the presence of apostasy, when men had to stand for God *and His honour*.

Or take a simple illustration. A father and son are both in the same assembly. Outside the assembly they are father and son; inside the assembly they are *brothers* IN CHRIST. Human arrangements and natural links must not obtrude in the things of God.

On the other hand "the Salt of the Covenant" had not to be lacking from the Offering. There should be that element present that would neutralize what would make for moral putrefaction, even the active purifying effect of the grace of God working in our hearts through the Word, and the practical application of the death of Christ applied to our hearts and consciences. The activities of that grace may not always be agreeable to us, but the effect is according to God's Covenant of blessing towards His own. "No chastening for the present seemeth to be joyous, but grievous; nevertheless afterward it yieldeth the peaceable fruit of righteousness unto them which are exercised thereby" (Hebrews 12:11).

GREEN EARS DRIED BY FIRE

The Meat Offering could take the form of Firstfruits unto the LORD, green ears dried by the fire, even corn beaten out of full ears, with oil and frankincense laid upon it. This all refers typically to Christ. There can be no spiritual harvest save through Christ. We recall the well-known Scripture, "Except a corn of wheat fall into the ground and die, it abideth alone: but if it die, it bringeth forth much fruit" (John 12:24). Again, "Now is Christ risen from the dead and become the *Firstfruits* of them that slept" (1 Corinthians 15:20).

How do the green ears set forth Christ? Notice that the ears were *green*, yet they were *full ears*, that is, they were mature. Does this not remind us of the prophet's wonderful lament, "I said, O my God, take Me not away in the midst of My days" (Psalm 102:24)? At about the age of thirty-three our Lord's life was cut off. And yet though He was, as to His manhood, but a young man (as men reckon), He was marked by full maturity. Though green the ears were full ears. Only three-and-a-half years covered His public ministry, and yet how profound a mark He has made on the world's history.

Further, these green ears, full ears of corn, were dried by fire. Does this not bring before us most touchingly, that the perfect life of our Lord was laid down at the cross? Oil poured upon the dried and beaten-out ears, with oil and frankincense put upon the Offering, signify that our Lord's life, laid down in death, was fragrant and delightful to the heart of God (*frankincense*). We get the Meat Offering as well as the Burnt Offering alluded to in Ephesians 5:2, where we read, "Walk in love as Christ also hath loved us, and hath given Himself for us an Offering and a Sacrifice to God for a sweet smelling savour." This memorial was burned upon the altar, "an offering made by fire unto the LORD."

Chapter 18:
The Peace Offering

READ LEVITICUS **3:1-17; 7:11-34**

Let it be at once observed that the Peace Offering was not an offering to *make peace*, but an offering that celebrated and rejoiced in *peace already made*. As another [J. N. Darby] has said, "It is the offering which typifies to us the communion of saints, according to the efficacy of the sacrifice with God, with the priest who has offered it in our behalf, with one another, and with the whole body of saints as priests to God." The blood of the sacrifice had indeed to be sprinkled round about the Altar. It is on the ground of shed blood alone that the communion of saints as to the death of Christ is based. The believer appropriates the Sin Offering first, and then being set free in conscience, he can joyfully enter into common thoughts with God about the wondrous sacrifice of His blessed Son, as typified in the Peace Offering.

A female as well as a male was admissible in this Offering, since its aspect was not so wholly for God as the Burnt Offering was, when only a male could be offered. Turtle doves or young pigeons were not admissible. It presupposes some strength of feeling that would lead the offerer to come forward with a Peace Offering.

Leviticus 7:12-13 shows that the Offering could take the form of a thanksgiving, or of a vow, or voluntary offering. This fully supports our explanation that this offering is not a question of peace to be made, but the enjoyment and thanksgiving for peace already made.

The offerer laid his hands on the head of the Offering, type of the believer's appropriation of Christ, and his identification with Him. The blood was sprinkled upon the Altar round about. The fat parts of the animal, that which speaks of inward power and strength, were burned upon the Altar, surely teaching there can be no communion apart from the death of Christ.

Leviticus 7:12-13 shows that when this Offering was presented as a thanksgiving, a Meat Offering might accompany it, thus showing how one aspect of Christ's death touches another aspect. It is impossible in such a theme, concerning such a Person and such a work, to place one aspect of Christ's death, as it were, in a watertight compartment. Thoughts of Christ's death lead us to the contemplation of His wondrous life; and the contemplation of His wondrous life leads us to worshipful meditation on His death.

As to this Meat Offering we read, "Besides the cakes, he shall offer for his offering *leavened* bread with the sacrifice of thanksgiving of his Peace Offerings" (Leviticus 7:13). There is one other occasion where *leaven* is brought in in connection with the offerings to the Lord. This is the New Meat Offering (Leviticus 23:17). Apart from these two exceptions, and of Amos 4:5, offering of *unleavened* bread is always emphasized.

It would be well to explain why this is so at this juncture, though it is anticipating in measure what we shall say when we speak of the Feasts of the Lord (Leviticus 23).

In Leviticus 7:13 we read that the leavened bread was offered with the Sacrifice of Thanksgiving. Here it is what *the Offerer presents* to God in the way of thanksgiving. The previous verse insists on *unleavened* bread and *unleavened* wafers. Is there any contradiction here?

Far be the thought. In the case of unleavened bread and unleavened wafers, both are typical of our blessed Lord, and therefore had to be *unleavened* to set forth the Lord's perfect freedom from sin in thought, word and deed. But if it is a question of OUR offering a thanksgiving sacrifice, the presence of leaven is but the acknowledgment that in OUR offering there may be ignorance, self-complacency, pride, lack of becoming reverence, even of rivalry. It is painful to hear defective or erroneous things said in thanksgiving, or to see a brother standing to a worship hymn with his hand in his pocket, or sitting in a careless lounging attitude. If they were in the presence of their earthly King, or President, there would be care and right reverence given in everything.

Surely the Spirit of God removes the leaven from the offering when presented to God. It is encouraging to know that, however failing our presentation to God of praise and thanksgiving may be, God delights to be thus approached.

We read that the offerer of a Peace Offering with "his own hands shall bring the offerings of the LORD made by fire" (Leviticus 7:30), showing how *individual* exercise has to be present on such an occasion as in communion approaching God concerning the sacrifice of our blessed Lord on the cross.

The offerer had to bring the fat with the breast, that "the breast may be waved for a Wave Offering before the LORD." The fat was burned upon the Altar, and the breast became the portion of Aaron and his sons. Similarly the right shoulder was a Heave Offering to the LORD, and became the portion of the offering priest.

What do we learn from the Breast, the Wave Offering, and the Shoulder, the Heave Offering? It is very sweet that what is presented to God, the Breast waved (Leviticus 7:30) is typical of the holy affections of our Lord, leading Him through death, and appreciated by His Father with infinite delight, and is also the communion of saints: God's full portion and ours. The Shoulder heaved speaks of the strength of the sacrifice, how the one supreme sacrifice of our Lord has once and for ever set us in the presence of God in cloudless favour. The right shoulder was the portion of the priest who offered the blood of the Peace Offering (Leviticus 7:33), thus setting forth our joy in communion as we think of the death of Christ.

This is seen very happily in that wonderful meeting when the saints gather to remember the Lord in His death. The Lord gets His portion, the Father gets His, as His Son is well spoken of, we get our portion, and what a wonderful portion it is. The one loaf speaks of communion embracing the whole Church of God. The Wave Offering goes up to God, the appreciation of the wonderful love of our Lord that took Him to the cross; the Heave Offering is heaved up, the appreciation of the strength of that sacrifice that can take us from the power of darkness and translate us into the kingdom of the Son of His love.

Finally, in the case of a vow or a voluntary offering, the food of the Peace Offering had to be eaten the same day, and if any remained to the third day, it had to be burned with fire. Anyone eating it the third day would commit an abomination against the LORD, and would have to bear his iniquity.

This teaches us that we must take our place in the worship of the Lord in the power and strength of *present* communion. It is a serious thing to profess to go into the Lord's presence, if not in communion of soul.

This is still further emphasized when Leviticus ends with a solemn warning, that if a soul eats of the sacrifice of the Peace Offering having uncleanness upon him, that soul shall be cut off from among his people. We get an example of this when we read of the Corinthian believers turning the Lord's hallowed supper into an occasion for surfeiting and drunkenness. We read, "For this cause many are weak and sickly among you, and many sleep" (1 Corinthians 11:30); that is, many were hindered from the partaking of the Lord's supper, and in extreme cases many died under the hand of God in judgment. *Fit* for glory they were by the grace of God and the atoning sacrifice of Christ; *unfit* for earthly testimony for Christ, and removed in discipline, but all that they "should not be condemned with the world." How God does insist on personal holiness on the part of those who have to do with the holy things of the Lord.

Chapter 19:
The Sin Offering

READ **LEVITICUS 4**

The Sin and Trespass Offerings were in reality both Sin Offerings, but each has its distinctive character, as we shall see.

In those we have been considering, Sweet Savour Offerings, we have before us offerings presented by one in communion approaching God. The Sin and Trespass Offerings set forth the approach to God of the sinner, or in the case of the Trespass Offering of one who has sinned against his neighbour. The Sweet Savour Offerings were burned *upon the Brazen Altar*.

The Sin Offerings were burned *"outside the camp"*.

It was the blood of the Sin Offering on the Great Day of Atonement that was carried by the High Priest into the Holiest of All, and sprinkled on and before the Mercy Seat. This alone is sufficient to show how solemn and important was this Offering.

The Sin Offering was required for sins committed in ignorance against any of the commandments of the Lord. The offerer was held guilty, whether he knew of the sin or not. Indeed "a sin of ignorance" supposed no knowledge of the offence. An offering presented supposed subsequent enlightenment.

How true it is that none of us really grasps the full seriousness of sin, that much, very much, God holds us guilty of, we are ignorant of. Does it not show how sin has beclouded our vision, and stultified our moral sensibilities?

And is it not happy to know, that if we pass over much in ourselves as right when it is wrong, God does not? In the light of *His* knowledge of what sin is, sin has been dealt with in full completeness at the cross of Calvary. With what relief of conscience we read such a statement as "The blood of Jesus Christ His Son cleanseth us from ALL sin" (1 John 1:7).

The Sin Offerings of Leviticus 4 are enumerated as follows:

1. *The sin of the anointed priest.*
2. *The sin of the whole congregation.*
3. *The sin of a ruler.*
4. *The sin of one of the common people.*

An examination of the differences in the way these sins are met, will show that the greater the privilege, the greater the responsibility, the greater the sin. In the case of "the priest that is anointed", or of "the whole congregation of Israel" that is guilty, a young bullock in either case had to be offered, and it had to be burned outside the camp. In either case the whole congregation was affected, for the anointed priest stood in relation to the whole camp.

If a ruler sinned it sufficed that he brought a kid of the goats, but it had to be a *male*, showing that the sin of a ruler was more serious than the sin of a common person.

If one of the common people sinned, he must bring a kid of the goats, in this case a *female* sufficed.

Thus we see that privilege, position, and nearness to God, made any ignorance, or sin arising therefrom, serious in proportion to the greatness of the privilege and position.

For instance, if an ordinary person broke some law of the land, it would be serious, but if a judge did so, the offence would be still more serious, for a judge ought to know what the laws of the land are. It is known in earthly courts for men to be fined for offences, when they were unaware that they had trespassed in any way. The law presupposes that men should be acquainted with its enactments. It is well for believers to study the Scriptures, so that they may not sin through ignorance.

If an anointed priest sinned "according to the sin of the people", he was instructed to bring a young bullock to the Door of the Tabernacle, lay his hand on the head of the sacrifice, and slay it before the LORD. The priest was then to take the blood, and dipping his finger therein sprinkle it seven times before the LORD before the vail of the Sanctuary, and put some of the blood on the horns of the Altar of Sweet Incense.

As the sinning priest did all this would he not feel how very serious it was for him to disobey the commandments of the LORD? He would realize how in his position as an anointed priest he had brought great dishonour on the name of the LORD.

The blood was poured out at the bottom of the Altar of Burnt Offering. The blood signified the life. Nothing less than the shedding of blood, the life surrendered under the judgment of God, would suffice to meet God's claims. Sin is a very serious matter, and all this ritual would bring it vividly home to the anointed, sinning priest.

The fat parts were then removed, and burned on the Altar of Burnt Offering, showing that even in this most solemn presentation of the death of Christ, there was that in the Offering that was supremely the delight of God, the surrender of our Lord's will, the deep hidden devotedness of Christ that led Him to such a death, all this was acceptable to God in fullest measure.

But now came the most solemn part of the ceremony. The skin of the bullock, its flesh, its head, its legs and inwards, its dung, the priest had to carry outside the camp to a clean place, where the ashes were poured out, and there burn the whole on the wood with fire. Surely the mind of the priest would feel deeply the seriousness of all this. The camp was a large place. Six hundred thousand men able to bear arms, besides old men and youths, women and children, were encamped round the Tabernacle. It must have been a solemn testimony as to what God thought about sin. A distance of six or seven miles lay between the Tabernacle and "outside the camp" where the ashes were poured out.

Scripture itself tells us the typical meaning of this. We read, "For the bodies of those beasts, whose blood is brought into the Sanctuary by the High Priest for sin, are burned *without the camp*. Wherefore Jesus also, that He might sanctify the people with His own blood, suffered *without the gate*" (Hebrews 13:11-12). Dying under the wrath of God because of our sins, uttering the bitterest of cries, "My God, My God, why hast Thou forsaken Me?" our Lord fulfilled the type of the Sin Offering in all its terrible meaning. Surely our souls may well bow before Him in deepest worship and thanksgiving, that He has met all the claims of Divine justice against us, and saved us from an eternal hell.

The different parts of the Sin Offering are enumerated, and call for our reverent meditation.

"The skin of the bullock", that which constituted its beauty, comes first under notice. Being burned typified that the glory of man in the flesh, that which between man and man is admired and gloried in, is obnoxious to God. "An high look, and a proud heart, and the plowing of the wicked is sin" (Proverbs 21:4).

"All his flesh" typified sin in general.

"With his head" signified plainly that every thought of sinful man is only evil in God's holy sight. "Every imagination of the thoughts of his [*man's*] heart was only evil continually" (Genesis 6:5).

"With his legs" signified that every activity of the natural man is sin. Where does sin come from? From a nature, and nature can only express itself. "They are all gone out of the way, they are together become unprofitable; there is none that doeth good, no, not one" (Romans 3:12).

"And his inwards" set forth that which was hidden and secret. Every movement of the natural heart and will is against God. The outside may look fair, but what of the inside? We "make clean the outside of the cup and of the platter, but *within* they are full of extortion and excess" (Matthew 23:25).

"And his dung" typified that which is outwardly vile and evil. Even sinful men condemn these grossly vile things that men are guilty of.

This description carries us irresistibly to the sweeping condemnation of man in the flesh as summed up in

Romans 3, where throat and tongue, and lips and mouth and feet are all members of wickedness. Isaiah adds his testimony, "From the sole of the foot even unto the head there is no soundness in it; but wounds and bruises and putrifying sores" (Isaiah 1:6). Again, "We are all as an unclean thing, and all our righteousnesses are as filthy rags" (Isaiah 64:6).

In these details we get the most solemn sense of what sin is, and of the unutterable woe that the Lord Jesus, the Son of God, had to face to meet our terrible need.

> *"He passed through death's dark raging flood*
> *To make our peace secure."*

Chapter 20:
The Trespass Offering

READ **LEVITICUS 5:1-19; 6:1-7**

We come now to the Trespass Offering, which is concerned mainly with specific and overt acts, some done in ignorance, some done knowingly. If a man was put upon his oath, and failed to give true evidence of what he had seen or heard of another's guilt, he was guilty, and a Trespass Offering was demanded. If a man touched an unclean thing, and though it was hidden from him, he was unclean and guilty. If one touched the uncleanness of man, and if it was hidden from him, when he knew of it, then he was guilty. If a man swore to do good or to do evil, and it was hid from him, when he knew of it, he was guilty in one of these.

A Trespass Offering was then needed. A *female* from the flock, or if the offender were too poor to furnish a sheep or a goat, he was allowed to offer two turtle doves or two young pigeons.

It is interesting to see that when two birds were offered, one was looked upon as a Sin Offering, the other as a Burnt Offering, thus showing that it is the death of Christ in all its aspects that is for the believer's blessing. In the

169

case here the Sin Offering came first, and then the Burnt Offering, thus following the order in which the sinner realizes the value of the death of Christ. First the Sin Offering, typifying *clearance*; then the Burnt Offering, typifying *acceptance*.

And then follows a most touching and extraordinary provision. If a man was so poor that even a pair of turtle doves or two young pigeons were beyond his power to provide, he was permitted to bring as a Trespass Offering the tenth part of an ephah of flour, a handful of which was burned on the Altar by the priest to make atonement for the specific sin committed, the remnant belonging to the priest as a Meat Offering.

Here is a Sin Offering *without blood*. What can it signify? One thing is certain. We know that from God's side everything for blessing for the sinner rests on the precious blood of Christ, and in no other way.

The explanation is simple and yet profound. It was a question of the offerer's extreme poverty, typical of one with a very feeble and vague sense of sin, and the way it can be met.

Many a soul is drawn, we believe, to the Lord with practically little or no knowledge of the real meaning of Christ's death, yet trusting Him in a vague and childlike manner for blessing and eternal happiness, and from such a type as this we are encouraged to believe that such a case is met by the death of Christ.

In the Old Testament times there were saints of God, who never knew of Christ, nor the full meaning of the death of Christ as dimly set forth in the Offerings, and yet, believing in God, they were blessed in view of the Sacrifice that was to be. We get the contrast between the Old Testament believers and those of this dispensation in the following, "God hath set forth [*Christ*] to be a propitiation through faith in His blood, to declare His righteousness for the remission of sins that are past through the forbearance of God", that is, the sins of Old Testament believers were passed over and forgiven in view of righteousness being met in due time by the atoning death of Christ. And now for the New Testament believers we read, "To declare, I say, *at this time* His righteousness: that He might be just, and the Justifier of Him which believeth in Jesus" (Romans 3:25-26).

We repeat most emphatically the words of Scripture, "Without shedding of blood is no remission" (Hebrews 9:22). Thank God, for this gracious provision that is made typically for those, who have vague and feeble apprehension, or who are ignorant of the Gospel as we know it, and yet whose souls are honestly stretching out to God and looking to Him for salvation, and finding it, even if unknown to themselves, in the atoning sacrifice of Christ on the cross.

The rest of the examples in this chapter, viz., a sin in *the holy things of the* LORD, or against any of the commandments of the LORD, though in ignorance, bring in a new element, viz. restitution.

A Ram was to be brought as a Trespass Offering. The principal, that is the equivalent of the fraud committed, was demanded, but added to it was to be a fifth part in addition. Where fraud had taken place, restitution was a most wholesome test of repentance, and any attempt to evade it, would mean that the priest could not offer the Trespass Offering, for the Offering and the restitution had to go together.

In Leviticus 6:1-7, where the sins were clearly breaches against a neighbour, the restitution comes first, and then the Offering. In the case of these breaches it was imperative to get right with the one sinned against, a right and urgent matter in the sight of God, before getting right with God Himself.

Chapter 21:
The Great Day of Atonement

READ LEVITICUS 16

The Great Day of Atonement was celebrated annually on the tenth day of the seventh month. It was designed typically to put the whole of the people of Israel in relationship with God on the ground of redemption. It did nothing *vitally*, any more than the blood of bulls and goats could put away sin. It was repeated again and again for the simple reason that the shadow could do nothing save point the way to what would be efficacious, till the time came when Christ "entered in ONCE into the Holy Place, having obtained *eternal redemption* for us" (Hebrews 9:12).

The vail was never rent under the shadows. But now, blessed be God, since Christ has died,

> *"The vail is rent, our souls draw near*
> *Unto a throne of grace.*
> *The merits of the Lord appear,*
> *They fill the Holy Place."*

The early breakdown of the priesthood in the case of Aaron's sons, Nadab and Abihu, who offered strange fire against God's commandment, when fire came down from the LORD and devoured them, and they died before the LORD, had a special reaction as we shall now see.

In Leviticus 16:2, we read that because of this breakdown, God forbad Aaron going at all times into the Holy Place within the vail before the Mercy Seat, that he die not. Very clear instructions were given when and how he was to enter, and that only on the Great Day of Atonement. "Into the second [viz., *the Holiest of All*] went the High Priest *alone* once every year, NOT WITHOUT BLOOD, which he offered for himself, and for the errors of the people; the Holy Ghost this signifying, that the way into the Holiest of All was not yet made manifest, while as the first Tabernacle was yet standing" (Hebrews 9:7-8).

Whilst in a general way this solemn ritual sets forth the truth and need of atonement, it will have a special fulfilment with Israel in a future day. This we shall see when we consider the Feasts of the LORD in a future chapter.

No longer was Aaron allowed to put on the garments of glory and beauty on this occasion. Arrayed in the inner linen garment, setting forth holiness, and washed with clean water, typical of moral fitness, Aaron took up his solemn office on the Great Day of Atonement.

He was instructed to furnish himself with a young bullock for a Sin Offering and a Ram for a Burnt Offering. This bullock was offered as a Sin Offering FOR HIMSELF and *his house*. In this he stands, not as a type, but as a contrast to our blessed Lord. Aaron and his house needed a Sin Offering, for they were sinners. Christ needed no Sin Offering, nay was Himself the Sin Offering, the perfect Sacrifice, who has glorified God at the cross.

Aaron took two kids of the goats for a Sin Offering, and one ram for a Burnt Offering of the congregation of the children of Israel. He then brought the two goats, and presented them before the LORD at the Door of the Tabernacle of the congregation. He then cast lots upon the two goats, one lot for the LORD and the other for the scapegoat.

And just at this point we find Aaron was instructed to slay the bullock for a Sin Offering for himself and his house, taking a censer full of burning coals from off the Altar. His hands filled with sweet incense beaten small, he put the incense upon the fire before the LORD so that the cloud of the incense covered the Mercy Seat that was upon the Testimony that he died not.

"That he die not", shows how intensely solemn the whole approach to God was. Nothing short of the atoning work of our Lord can give us title to be in God's presence. It is a relief to turn from self to Christ, and find in HIM our righteousness in God's presence.

Then Aaron took of the blood of the bullock, and sprinkled it with his finger upon the Mercy Seat eastward, and before the Mercy Seat seven times.

After that he killed the goat of the Sin Offering that was for the people, and did with the blood of the goat what he had done with the blood of the bullock, sprinkling its blood on the Mercy Seat. Thus he made atonement for the Holy Place, and for the uncleanness of the children of Israel, and for the Tabernacle that was in the midst of their uncleanness. No man accompanied him in doing this. He then came out and proceeded to the Brazen Altar, took the blood of the bullock and the blood of the goat, and sprinkled seven times the Altar and hallowed it from uncleanness. Thus year by year would the children of

Israel be reminded of the holiness of God, and the necessity of a sufficient and accepted sacrifice.

We can clearly see the connection between the Throne and the Altar, the Altar meeting the claims of the Throne. In the very highest way the blood of Christ met every claim of God in fullest satisfaction; nay, it glorified Him where sin had brought in dishonour, glorified Him as nothing else could.

Let it ever be remembered, the believer can go as far as the blood went. The blood could go no further. It went into the very presence of God, turning a Throne of inflexible righteousness (and for ever remaining so) into a Mercy Seat. "Christ also hath once suffered for sins, the Just for the unjust, that *He might bring us* TO GOD" (1 Peter 3:18).

The blood was sprinkled once upon the Mercy Seat, and seven times before it; *once* for God, that sufficed fully, seeing He alone can fully estimate the wonderful efficacy of the precious atoning work of our Lord on the cross; *seven* times for us, who need to be assured again and again of these things. It is not all at once that we grasp the full meaning of the precious blood of Christ. As time goes on we come into a fuller and growing appreciation of that work till we find ourselves in the presence of the Lord when our praises shall be eternal. "Unto Him that loved us, and washed us from our sins in His own blood, and hath made us kings and priests unto God and His Father; to Him be glory and dominion for ever and ever. Amen" (Revelation 1:5-6). Thank God we stand before Him in the measure of *His* appreciation of Christ's work on the cross, not of *ours*.

And now what about the two goats Aaron was instructed to take for the people? We have seen how the goat that was the LORD's lot was slain, but the live goat is seen as being identified with the slain goat whose blood was sprinkled on the Mercy Seat. We quote two verses to make this plain. "And Aaron shall bring the goat upon which the LORD's lot fell, and offer him for a Sin Offering. But the goat, on which the lot fell to be the scapegoat, shall be presented alive before the LORD to make an atonement with him, and to let him go for a scapegoat into the wilderness" (Leviticus 16:9-10). The two goats are identified one with the other, and carry one great lesson.

Upon the head of the live goat, in virtue of what is set forth typically in the death of the goat which was the LORD's lot, the High Priest laid his hands, and confessed the iniquities of the children of Israel, and all their transgressions, putting them in that symbolic way on the head of the goat, and then sent him away by the hands of a fit man into the wilderness. In this highly spectacular way was typified how thoroughly sin is put away—clean gone, never to be seen again. It reminds us of Scriptures that show how thoroughly God deals with sin. We read, "As far as the east is from the west, so far hath He removed our transgressions from us" (Psalm 103:12). "Thou wilt cast all their sins into the depths of the sea" (Micah 7:19). "Thou hast cast all my sins behind Thy back" (Isaiah 38:17). "Their sins and iniquities will I remember no more" (Hebrews 10:17).

Whilst all this may be a comfort and assurance to the individual believer, and rightly so, yet the goat going into the wilderness with the sins of the nation confessed on its head, typified *specifically* what will happen to Israel in a future day. As the result of the repentance wrought by the spirit of grace and supplications being poured out upon the Jewish nation, in that day when they shall look upon Him whom they have pierced (see Zechariah 12:10) they will then keep the Feast of the Great Day of Atonement as they have never kept it in all their long history, and will read in this spectacular ritual, having Christ then as the key to it all, how sin has been effectually put away. Just as the let-go goat disappeared in the wilderness to be seen no more, so the blood of the Sin Offering, even the precious blood of the Christ they despised and cast out, they will see to be efficacious before God for their full and complete redemption, and "their sins and iniquities will I remember no more" (Hebrews 10:17) will be the assurance of the Lord to them according to the covenant of grace made with Israel.

It was when Aaron came out of the Holy Place that the scapegoat was sent into the wilderness; and it will be when Christ shall come again to earth, and Israel purified through the great Tribulation, and repentant, shall welcome their Messiah, that this precious type will meet its fulfilment. Meanwhile Christ is hidden, and His people of this dispensation have their portion with Him,* "blessed … with all spiritual blessings in heavenly places in Christ" (Ephesians 1:3).

NOTE

* The Seventh Day Adventists teach that the scapegoat is Satan, that Christ will remove from the heavenly Sanctuary the sins of His people, and will place them upon Satan. "As the scapegoat was sent into an uninhabited land never to come into the congregation again, so will Satan be banished from God's presence to be blotted out of existence in the final destruction of sin and sinners." This teaching is pure assumption, a blasphemous contradiction of our Lord's triumphant words on the cross, "IT IS FINISHED." To teach that Christ is now making atonement in Heaven, and that at the end Satan is called upon to finish the work and be annihilated in the end, is the strangest bit of exegesis we have ever heard. The Hebrew word for scapegoat is *Azazel*, meaning a goat for going away. The word occurs four times in Leviticus 16, and nowhere else in Scripture, and does not refer to Satan by any stretch of fancy.

Aaron, having let the live goat go into the wilderness by the hand of the fit man, then came into the Tabernacle of the Congregation, put off his linen garments, washed his flesh with water in the Holy Place, put on his garments of glory and beauty, and came forth and offered his own Burnt Offering, and that for the people. Then Aaron's bullock, and the goat, the LORD's lot, already slain, were carried outside the camp and there burned in the fire—skins, flesh and dung—figure of God's unsparing judgment on sin at the cross. But even in that solemn type the fat was burned upon the Altar of Burnt Offering, there was ever that which was delightful to the heart of God in the blessed redemption His Son made for sin.

This completed the ritual on the Great Day of Atonement, a most precious type of the atoning death of our Lord Jesus Christ.

KEY WORDS IN THE EPISTLE TO THE HEBREWS

In the light of what we have been considering, it is interesting to note the key words of the Epistle to the Hebrews, key words used to contrast the glorious fullness of Christ, the Antitype, with the ineffectual shadows.

"BETTER" IS ONE KEY WORD—

Christ "… better than the Angels" (1:4); "a better hope" (7:19); "a better Testament" (7:22); "a better Covenant" (8:6); "better promises" (8:6); "better sacrifices" (9:23); "a better country" (11:16); "a better … substance" (10:34); "a better resurrection" (11:35). Grammarians will tell you that "better" is comparative, but never was such a superlative comparative used, if we may employ such a phrase.

"ONCE", OR "ONE", IS ANOTHER KEY WORD—

"Christ was once offered to bear the sins of many" (9:28); "once for all" (10:10); "one sacrifice for sins" (10:12);

"one offering" (10:14)—in contrast to the unending succession of sacrifices under the law, which could never take away sin.

"NO MORE" IS ANOTHER KEY PHRASE—

"no more conscience of sins" (10:2); "no more sacrifice for sins" (10:26)—this is just another way of showing forth the complete efficacy of Christ's work upon the cross.

"ETERNAL" IS ANOTHER KEY WORD—

"eternal salvation" (5:9); "eternal judgment" (6:2); "eternal redemption" (9:12); "eternal Spirit" (9:14); "eternal inheritance" (9:15). To these might be added "an unchangeable priesthood". "And they truly were many priests, because they were not suffered to continue by reason of death: but this Man, because He continueth ever, hath an unchangeable priesthood" (Hebrews 7:23-24).

Thus is contrasted the stability, permanence and perfection of Divine things with the temporary, unsatisfactory character of carnal ordinances. The glorious Substance, the great Antitype, the Lord Jesus, has arrived, and the shadows have fled away. That is the poverty and blindness of present day ritualism, copying the shadows when all the time the true meaning of them is unknown. The greater the ritualism the less the spiritual life. Christ is the key to the meaning of these types. How can any, who really know the Antitype, go back to shadows in which God had no pleasure (Hebrews 10:6).

Chapter 22:
The Cleansing of the Leper

READ LEVITICUS 13 AND 14

Leprosy is a terrible figure of sin. All disease is the result of sin, but the incurable character of leprosy, the terrible way it disfigures its victims, how first one joint and then another of fingers and toes are eaten away, nose eaten off, hair falling out, till the poor sufferer looks a pitiable object, makes it a striking figure of sin in its defiling ineradicable and contagious nature [11]. Moreover it is so contagious that the victim must be segregated from his fellows.

The first mention of leprosy in the Bible was when the Lord told Moses to thrust his hand into his bosom, and when drawn out "his hand was leprous as snow" (Exodus 4:6), as if to show the truth of the prophet's utterance, "From the sole of the foot even unto the head there is no soundness in it; but wounds, and bruises, and putrifying sores; they have not been closed, neither bound up, neither mollified with ointment" (Isaiah 1:6).

Leviticus 13 gives a very careful diagnosis of the disease, so that the priest could decide whether a man was a leper or not. One spot with certain characteristics would decide the leprosy of the individual. One spot reveals an inward diseased condition, just as one sin comes from a sinful nature. How good God is in giving us such a vivid presentation of what sin is in His presence. One spot might disclose the leper, but on the other hand if the whole body wherever looked at by the priest was covered with leprosy from head to foot, "then the priest shall consider: and, behold, if the leprosy have covered all his flesh, he shall pronounce him clean that hath the plague: it is all turned white: he is clean" (Leviticus 13:13). This seems to teach that when a sinner really owns fully his sinnership, it is then the mercy of God can come in, and bless him. Job in the Old Testament and Saul of Tarsus in the New Testament come to mind in this connection.

Job was a wonderful man, upright, perfect in his ways, generous, looked up to with deep respect by old and young, and then challenged by Satan, the Lord allowed him to be stripped of wealth and family in one day, to be tormented by boils from head to foot, to be tortured and irritated by his three carping friends, charging him with being a hypocrite, which he certainly was not. At last when God spoke to him he came most astonishingly to the true estimate of himself in God's presence. "I have heard of Thee by the hearing of the ear, but now mine eye seeth Thee. Wherefore I abhor myself, and repent in dust and ashes" (Job 42:5-6). Would Job ever forget that day? It was the best day of his life. The leprosy had covered all his flesh. It had all turned white. He was clean. The leprosy had worked out in the flesh till there was no more flesh to work upon, and he was thus clean.

Take Saul of Tarsus. What a good show in the flesh he made. He was sincere, if ever a man was. As touching the righteousness of the law he was blameless. But one day he got a vision of Christ. He saw a light above the brightness of the sun. He was stricken down, and learned in a moment that the One he was opposing, in savagely haling His humble followers to prison, and hounding them to death, was none less than the Son of God, a glorious Saviour, risen and triumphant at God's right hand. He took up his pen and wrote, "This is a faithful saying, and worthy of all acceptation, that Christ Jesus came into the world to save sinners; *of whom* I AM CHIEF" (1 Timothy 1:15). The leprosy covered all his flesh. He was clean.

Of course we must be careful at this point. The flesh, the fallen evil nature with which we are born, is ever the flesh. There will be no cure for that. "If we say that we have no sin, we deceive ourselves, and the truth is not in us" (1 John 1:8), though the verse before says so beautifully and truly that "the blood of Jesus Christ, His Son, cleanseth us from ALL sin."

The type goes no further than a sinner fully realizing his sinnership, and owning his true condition before God, being looked at as clean in God's holy sight, though we know full well that it is only through the atoning sacrifice of Christ that blessing can come to any.

When a man was pronounced a leper how pitiable was his condition. We read, "The leper in whom the plague is, his clothes shall be rent, and his head bare, and he shall put a covering upon his upper lip, and shall cry, Unclean, Unclean. All the days wherein the plague shall be in him he shall be defiled; he is unclean; he shall dwell alone: without the camp shall his habitation be" (Leviticus 13:45-46).

Not only was the leper segregated as an individual, but he was cut off from the Congregation. Is this not typical of sin cutting a soul off from communion with God? It may be the sin of a believer is of such a nature as to cause him to be put away from the fellowship of saints on earth, as was the case of the incestuous man in 1 Corinthians 5. There is a "within" and "without" in relation to God's assembly, which is a place of holiness, where evil is to be judged and dealt with, when it occurs, just as there was a within and without in the camp of the Israelites.

In Leviticus 14 we read of a house being plagued with leprosy. When that was proved, the house had to be emptied, scraped and the dust taken into an unclean place. Other stones and plaster were then used, but if the plague broke out again, it is "a fretting leprosy" beyond recovery, and so the house must be broken down, stones, timber, plaster, and all carried to an unclean place.

Do we not know something of this to-day? Take these professing Christian bodies, who are unsound as to the Person of our Lord and His atoning death, have they not got "a fretting leprosy" in their midst? Take the case of Christadelphians, Seventh Day Adventists, Millennial Dawnists, Jehovah's Witnesses, Christian Scientists, and others, are they not all in similar condition, leprous houses? There is nothing for it but to refuse to have anything to do with such blasphemous anti-Christian systems. It is "a fretting leprosy".

The cleansing of the healed leper is most instructive typically. The priest commanded that two birds be taken alive and clean with cedar wood, scarlet and hyssop. One of the birds was to be killed in an earthen vessel over running water. The other living bird with the cedar wood and scarlet and hyssop was dipped in the blood of the bird that was killed over running water, and the blood sprinkled seven times upon the healed leper and the living bird let loose in the open field.

We pause here. How touching are these items typically. The slain bird is typical of our Lord, who died to cleanse us by His precious blood. The bird was killed in an earthen vessel. Our Lord who was very God of very God, God the eternal Son, became a Man, and thus came in "an earthen vessel". "A body hast Thou prepared Me" (Hebrews 10:5). The bird was killed over "running water". Water is typical of the word of God as applied by the Holy Spirit, and *running* water speaks of the Holy Spirit in *activity*. "Christ ... through the eternal Spirit offered Himself without spot to God" (Hebrews 9:14).

As to the living bird, it was identified with the slain bird, inasmuch as it was dipped in its blood. Let loose into the open field, allowed to fly to heaven, as it were, it set forth how our blessed Lord brought to death for our sins, rose triumphantly from the dead, and ascended to glory, the proof of the victory He had won. What a testimony! Just as the bird with blood-marked wings flew to the heavens, so we read of Christ, "Neither by the blood of goats and calves but by His own blood He entered in once into the Holy Place, having obtained eternal redemption for us" (Hebrews 9:12). Not only was the living bird dipped in the blood of the slain bird, but also the cedar wood, scarlet and hyssop. Cedar wood and scarlet speak of man in all his grandeur. Solomon spoke of trees, "From the cedar tree that is in Lebanon even unto the hyssop that springeth out of the wall" (1 Kings 4:33). The lowly stoop of our Lord from the throne of God to the manger of Bethlehem, to the cross of Calvary, puts into the dust all man's grandeur. Does not Isaac Watt's wonderful hymn show us the dipping in blood of the cedar wood and scarlet?

"When we survey the wondrous cross
  On which the Prince of glory died,
  Our richest gain we count but loss,
  And pour contempt on all our pride."

As to the hyssop, emblematical of that which is mean in nature, many think the poor should be blessed because of their sad lot in this life, but the blood-stained hyssop sets aside that notion. We are all sinners. It is all beautifully summed up by the dying King Edward VII, when he asked Prebendary Carlile, Founder of the Church Army, how his tramps were. Before the Prebendary had time to reply, the King said, "Take notice, Carlile, that tramps [hyssop] and Kings [cedar wood and scarlet] need the same Saviour." What a wonderful lesson for the King in all his exalted position to have learned!

Then there come the most elaborate details as to the cleansing, telling loudly that there must not only be done a work *outside* the sinner, but also *inside* the sinner, so that there may be the leaving off of all practical defilement. Holiness is insisted upon. Let the matter be crystal clear. It is the death and blood-shedding of our Lord on the cross, that gives the sinner, who believes, *title* before God—a title, not of works, but all of the grace of God, on the righteous ground that the atoning death of our Lord has settled the whole question of sin for the believing sinner. But on the other hand there must be *moral suitability*, or *fitness*, to be in God's presence.

There is not only the blood, but the water—blood, setting forth *judicial* cleansing, giving *title* to God's presence; the water, the cleansing action of the Word of God, giving *fitness*. Judicial standing first, then moral suitability. A peer of the realm may have title to appear at the King's Court, but he would never dream of appearing there in anything but court dress.

The healed leper was pronounced clean, but he had to wash his clothes, symbolic of a man coming under the influence of the grace of God giving up habits that are not suitable to his approach to God. The leper had to wash himself and shave off all his hair, setting forth something still more intimate as unfitting for God. For seven days he was to tarry out of his tent abroad. On the seventh day he had to shave the hair off his head, his beard and eyebrows, wash his clothes and himself again, and then he was clean. How God inculcates holiness in thought, talk, and ways of His beloved people.

On the eighth day the cleansed leper was to take two he lambs without blemish, one ewe lamb of the first year without blemish, three tenth deals of fine flour for a Meat Offering, mingled with oil and one log [12] of oil. The first thing that was done was to slay a lamb for a Trespass Offering, and wave it before the Lord. Then the priest took of the blood of the Sacrifice, and put it upon the right ear of him that was to be cleansed, upon the thumb of his right hand, and upon the great toe of his right foot. In this way was symbolized, first, that there is no approach to God save on the ground of the atoning sacrifice of our Lord, and second, that the amazing love of that Sacrifice claims from us nothing less than the consecration of our lives to Him, who loved us and gave Himself for us. "The love of Christ constraineth us; because we thus judge, that if One died for all, then were all dead; and that He died for all, that they which live should NOT *henceforth live unto themselves, but* UNTO HIM, which died for them and rose again" (2 Corinthians 5:14-15). Not only should there be a response on our side, but the glad acknowledgment of the claim that God makes on His side.

Now we see the reason for the log of oil. Some of the oil was poured into the palm of the priest's hand and with it he anointed the tip of the leper's right ear, the thumb of his right hand, and the great toe of his right foot. These members were already marked with blood. So the oil was put upon the blood. The ear is that which receives communications, the hand and foot carry them out. The oil is symbolic of the Holy Spirit, and that it is only in the strength and power of God's Holy Spirit that the believer will be able to respond in the way that is suitable to such Divine love and grace. The remnant of the oil was poured out upon the head of the cleansed leper, a picture of the whole man being claimed for God.

> *"Love so amazing, so Divine,*
> *Demands my soul, my life, my all."*

Then was offered a Sin Offering, followed by a Burnt Offering and a Meat Offering, as if to bring before the soul the different aspects of the death of Christ, showing what was needed to meet our deep need.

Chapter 23:
The Ashes of the Red Heifer

Read **Numbers 19**

Occurring in the Book of Numbers at the end of the wilderness experience of the children of Israel, it has a special significance. We shall see it is a provision for the removal of defilement from people already in association with a Holy God. It will teach believers a lesson to be vigilant as to our practical ways as Christians, and as to the associations we keep.

The children of Israel were to bring to Eleazar, the priest, a red heifer without spot or blemish and upon which never came yoke. Eleazar had to bring the heifer *outside the camp*, and one should slay her before his face. Then the priest with his finger had to sprinkle the blood, directly before the Tabernacle of the Congregation seven times, showing all in the Congregation are in view. The heifer was then burned in the sight of Eleazar—her skin, flesh, blood and dung—all had to be burned. Then Eleazar took cedar wood, scarlet and hyssop, and cast them into the burning. A clean man then gathered the ashes of the red heifer into a clean place without the camp, for the use of the whole congregation for "a water of separation; it is a purification for sin" (Numbers 19:9).

The meaning of all this is plain. There can be no holiness apart from the redemptive work of Christ, when at Calvary God showed His abhorrence of sin in that His full judgment upon sin was seen when He forsook the Sin-bearer, His only begotten Son, visiting Him with all the wrath sin deserved. The burning of the heifer in all its parts, whether it be its skin, the beauty of the animal, or the dung, the grossness of sin—all of man, his best as his worst—symbolizes the unsparing judgment of God in the person of the Substitute. Our Lord was without spot and blemish. "He knew no sin." "He did no sin." "In Him was no sin." So Scripture testifies. Upon Him never came yoke. He was completely free from sin and its penalty, else He could not have laid down His life for us.

The priest casting the cedar wood, hyssop and scarlet into the burning shows that all human pride and glory must go, the hyssop setting forth the meanness of man, all must go from top to bottom.

When a man was unclean by touching a dead body, his uncleanness was upon him for seven days. On the third day "he shall purify himself" by taking running water with the ashes of the heifer in a vessel, and be sprinkled therewith, and again on the seventh day. On the seventh day the unclean person having purified himself, washed his clothes, and bathed himself in water, at even he was pronounced clean.

The meaning of this is that when a believer is unclean through permitting sin and failure in his life, for purification there must be a sense of God's holiness as symbolized in the slaying and burning of the Red Heifer. Does the *Red* Heifer emphasize this? The ashes speak of the judgment on sin having been carried out. The remembrance of that, and the application of the Word in the cleansing power of the Holy Spirit of God, typified by the "running water" being mixed with the ashes (the recollection of what our Lord went through on the cross), have their own subduing, cleansing influence on the heart of the believer.

Not only so, but washing the clothes and washing the person set forth the defiled person's activity in putting out of his life defiling ways, or even thoughts, and the necessity of being personally clean in moral condition before God.

This sets forth not the cleansing of the sinner by *blood*, but of the saint by the *water* of the Word, engaging the heart with the solemn sense of sin as seen typically in the burning of the Sacrifice, and in the ashes, so that the heart of the believer really judges himself in the presence of God.

Mark what is said about the third day and the seventh day. There must be time for an erring saint to recover communion with God. For instance, if a preacher were caught in some evil sin, and he got restored, it would not be suitable for him to dash into prominence as a servant, but take time for full restoration.

This might be instanced in the case of the Apostle Peter. After his fall, denying His Lord with oaths and curses, our Lord looked upon him with that look of mingled grief and forgiving love, which made him go out and weep bitterly. But something further was needed. Our Lord saw Peter specially by himself after He rose from the dead. But still later the Lord probed him to the very bottom, till Peter uncovered his heart in the presence of the Lord, and exclaimed, "Lord, Thou knowest all things; Thou knowest that I love Thee" (John 21:17). Our Lord then gave him his commission, "Feed My sheep", and he was the spokesman on the great Day of Pentecost.

We do well to meditate upon this incident of the ashes of the Red Heifer, teaching us what a defiling thing sin is, and how necessary to be preserved in a state of fitness in God's holy presence. It shows, too, that a saint may not always contract defilement by his own act, but getting into touch with defilement, it may be even unwittingly, he is defiled, and needs the "water of purification". One may have to judge some sin in the assembly, and the mind be defiled listening to the sordid story, and a purification be needed. It says the ashes mixed with running water is "a water of separation". How necessary separation from evil is, and to be preserved in happy enjoyment of heart in communion with God.

Chapter 24:
Four Great Historical Types of the Death of Christ

READ 1 PETER 1:18-20; 1 CORINTHIANS 10:1-12; ROMANS 8:1-4; JOSHUA 3 AND 4; EPHESIANS 1:3-7

These four types are not intimately connected with the Tabernacle, but afford such striking lessons concerning the children of Israel, who were ranged round the Tabernacle in their journey to Canaan, that we have deemed it well to insert this chapter.

There are four great historical types of the death of Christ, as illustrated in the journey of the children of Israel from Egypt to Canaan. They were:—

1. *The Passover.*
2. *The Crossing of the Red Sea.*
3. *The Uplifting of the Brazen Serpent.*
4. *The Crossing of the Jordan into Canaan.*

Very briefly they can be described as follows:—

1. *The Passover,* typifying how God satisfied His claims in respect of sin, so that He could redeem His people righteously.

2. *The Crossing of the Red Sea*, typifying the deliverance of believers from Satan's power (Pharaoh), and from the bondage of the world (Egypt).

3. *The Uplifting of the Brazen Serpent*, typifying how the believer gets deliverance from the bondage of the flesh by the introduction of Divine life, and the indwelling of the Holy Spirit.

4. *The Crossing of the Jordan into Canaan*, typifying how the believer comes to be blessed "with all spiritual blessings in heavenly places in Christ" (Ephesians 1:3).

This bare outline we will now begin to amplify.

THE PASSOVER

Let it be particularly noted at the outset that the Passover is the only type of the four in which there was bloodshedding. The other three flow out of this first grand type, setting forth the great foundation of all our blessings, even the atoning work of our Lord Jesus Christ upon the cross of Calvary.

For after all how could there be any further action on God's part, if His righteous claims were not first met? And further, all God's subsequent actions in blessing His people are founded on this great outstanding start.

God was about to answer the groans of the oppressed children of Israel. But in order to do so, He must be *righteous*. The children of Israel were as much sinners as the Egyptians. What right had God to favour the children of Israel as against the Egyptians? The Egyptians as a nation had enslaved the children of Israel, and when God demanded that they should allow them to worship in the desert, Pharaoh refused. Therefore God in righteousness visited Egypt with His sore displeasure. If Pharaoh would not let the children of Israel go, God Himself would bring them forth out of Egypt "with a mighty hand, and with an outstretched arm, and with great terribleness, and with signs, and with wonders" (Deuteronomy 26:8). On the other hand God could only redeem His people by first meeting His own righteous claims. The great point to grasp in the Passover is, that it was the one great and vital question of a settlement with God. Other questions came in later, but this is the one great matter to be first settled.

We would now state in a couple of sentences the whole pith of the matter. *God shut Himself out as a righteous Judge, by bringing Himself in as a gracious yet righteous Saviour.* Of course this was all typical, but how rich is the type when we consider the Antitype.

A lamb without blemish had to be killed, its blood put into a basin, and with a bunch of hyssop the lintel and door posts of the houses, where the Israelites were, had to be sprinkled by blood, and Jehovah pledged His word that when He saw the blood He would *pass over*, hence the word, Passover. But in type it prefigures a *righteous* pass over. The blood of the lamb was but a type of the precious blood of Christ, which cleanseth from all sin. So we read in the New Testament, "Christ OUR PASSOVER is sacrificed for us" (1 Corinthians 5:7); "Forasmuch as ye know that ye were not redeemed with corruptible things as silver and gold, from your vain conversation received by tradition from your fathers; but with the precious blood of Christ, as of a lamb without blemish and without spot" (1 Peter 1:18-19).

In previous chapters we have written about the Passover, so will add no more here.

THE CROSSING OF THE RED SEA

Once God's righteous claims were met, and that by His own provision, there was still present the lamentable condition of the children of Israel. In the cruel grip of Pharaoh, a nation of slaves, making "bricks without straw", in the land of Egypt, could God leave a redeemed people in that plight? A further action followed out of the first great action, the Passover. What was needed was deliverance from Pharaoh and Egypt. Pharaoh is a type of *Satan*. So we read, "Forasmuch then as the children are partakers of flesh and blood, He [*Christ*] also Himself likewise took part of the same; that through death He might destroy him that had the power of death, that is, the Devil; and deliver them who through fear of death were all their lifetime subject to bondage" (Hebrews 2:14-15). Egypt is a type of *the world*. "And an angel of the LORD came up from Gilgal to Bochim, and said, I made you to go up out of Egypt, and have brought you unto the land which I sware unto your fathers; and I said, I will never break My covenant with you" (Judges 2:1). The believer though in the world is not of the world. Twice over in the ever-memorable prayer of our Lord breathed into His Father's ear, we read, "They are not of the world, even as I am not of the world" (John 17:14, 16). What a wonderful deliverance!

1 Corinthians 10:1-4 gives us a beautiful scriptural illustration of the typical meaning of the crossing of the Red Sea. The children of Israel passed through the Red Sea, that, which was death to the Egyptians, was for the Israelites the way of deliverance from Egypt and the bondage of Pharaoh. It must have been a terrible ordeal as the Egyptians in full-armed force threatened to annihilate them, hemming the Israelites in between Pi-hahiroth and Migdol and the sea. The case was desperate, but the sea in

front was cleft in two, and a path made through it by the mighty power of the God-sent east wind, and they passed safely through to the other side.

1 Corinthians 10 tells us how the children of Israel "were all baptized unto Moses in the cloud and in the sea", as if the wall of water on each side, and the cloud resting on the water, made a dark tunnel through which they passed. What a deliverance! No more Pharaoh, no more Egypt, and on the other side of the Red Sea they were under the leadership of Moses with heavenly resources in the stream, which flowed from the smitten rock for drink, and the daily manna for food. We are told distinctly that the Rock that followed them was Christ, the water flowing from the smitten rock being designated as the Rock that followed them.

The Passover brought out, as we have already seen, the thought of *the death of Christ* FOR *us*. The Crossing of the Red Sea *our* IDENTIFICATION *with that death*. The children of Israel were baptized unto Moses. Believers are baptized unto the death of Christ, they are buried with Him by baptism, and are now free to walk *in newness* OF LIFE. The death of Christ has freed believers from the power of Satan, and from the world as a system away from God, and committed them to Christ spirit, soul and body.

> *"From Egypt lately come,*
> *Where death and darkness reign,*
> *We seek our new, our better home,*
> *Where we our rest shall gain:*
> *Hallelujah!*
> *We are on our way to God."*

The Uplifting of the Brazen Serpent

Towards the end of the children of Israel's wandering in the desert, a remarkable incident occurred. The soul of the people was much discouraged by the way, they murmured against God and Moses, saying, "Wherefore have ye brought us up out of Egypt to die in the wilderness? For there is no bread, neither is there any water; and our soul loatheth this light bread [*manna*]" (Numbers 21:5). They murmured against the goodness of God, and despised His provision for them in giving them water from the flinty rock and "angels' food" (Psalm 78:25).

So "the LORD sent fiery serpents among the people, and they bit the people; and much people of Israel died" (Numbers 21:6). What lesson have we to learn from this incident? It is one that takes much learning and is a very necessary one. Sin springs from a sinful *nature*. What can thistles produce but thistles? "Ye shall know them by their fruits", said the Lord. "Do men gather grapes of thorns, or figs of thistles?" (Matthew 7:16).

The Passover taught the lesson of deliverance *from the judgment of God*. The crossing of the Red Sea taught deliverance *from Egypt (the world) and Pharaoh (Satan)*. The uplifting of the Brazen Serpent teaches the way of deliverance *from sinful self*. It is a deep and a practical lesson.

What was the remedy? Moses was instructed to make a Serpent of Brass, and those who looked would live. Have we any light thrown upon this in the New Testament? Most certainly we have. We read, "As Moses lifted up the serpent in the wilderness, even so must the Son of Man be lifted up; that whosoever believeth in Him should not perish, *but have eternal life*" (John 3:14-15). The Brazen Serpent is typical of our Lord being lifted up to die on the cross that sinful men might have *life*.

There are two grand results flowing from the death of Christ, as seen in 1 John 4:9-10. We read, "In this was manifested the love of God towards us, because that God sent His only begotten Son into the world, that we might LIVE THROUGH HIM. Herein is love, not that we loved God, but that He loved us, and sent His Son to be the PROPITIATION FOR OUR SINS." Not only the forgiveness of sins is ours, but DIVINE LIFE is imparted to every believer.

We read, "It came to pass, that if a serpent had bitten any man, when he beheld the Serpent of Brass, he LIVED" (Numbers 21:9). Just in the same way, the one who looks to Christ, once uplifted for our sins on the cross, that one will *live*. It is well seen that sinful flesh can only bring forth sin, and will never find a place in Heaven. As the child's hymn puts it,

> *"There is a city bright,*
> *Closed are its gates to sin;*
> *Naught that defileth,*
> *Naught that defileth*
> *Can ever enter in."*

All through John's Epistle the great theme is life! *Life!!* LIFE!!! The gospel is framed on the type of the Uplifted Brazen Serpent.

Romans 8:3-4 brings out the same truth, but in a different setting. We read, "What the law could not do, in that it was weak through the flesh, God sending His own Son in the likeness of sinful flesh, and for sin, condemned sin in the flesh: that the righteousness of the law might be fulfilled in us, who walk not after the flesh, but after the Spirit." The Brazen Serpent was in the likeness of the fiery serpent that bit the people, the Lord Jesus was in the likeness of sinful flesh. He was not sinful flesh, or else He could not have been our Saviour. Not only is sin atoned for, but sin in the flesh has been condemned in the death of our Lord Jesus Christ. Not only is the *fruit* (sins) dealt with, but also the *root* (sinful nature). Sins are forgiven. The sinful nature is not forgiven. That could never be. The only thing that will do for sin in the flesh is DEATH.

The great mistake of many in Christendom to-day is that they are trying to cultivate man in the flesh. If we tried to cultivate a thistle, we might be successful in producing bigger and more aggressive thistles, but we should only produce thistles. It is for the believer to recognize this, and to seek grace to "walk in the Spirit". The Apostle Paul speaks of "Newness of *Life*" (Romans 6:4). The Apostle John speaks of "Eternal *Life*" (John 3:15).

If once the teaching of the Brazen Serpent is apprehended, we shall learn that there is nothing in the flesh for God, that we cannot improve it, that we need to pass the sentence of death upon ourselves in this particular. It has been well said of the two natures they cannot be improved. The flesh is so bad it cannot be improved. The new nature is so good, it cannot be improved.

What a sight the uplifted Son of God must have been. What a lesson for us that not only has sin been atoned for, but the sinful nature has been condemned at the cross, and so if the Lord is to have a people in whom He can have pleasure, they must have a *life* to which no sin was ever attached, and the Holy Spirit of God must be given as the *power* for that new life, so that we "walk in the Spirit" (Galatians 5:25).

THE CROSSING OF THE JORDAN

READ JOSHUA 3 AND 4, AND EPHESIANS 1:3-5

The Crossing of the Jordan meant the end of the wilderness journey, and entrance into Canaan, the land flowing with milk and honey. There was fighting to do to possess the land and to turn out the enemy. We Christians are in the wilderness so far as our earthly circumstances are concerned. We have to face trials and difficulties of all kinds. But *in spirit* we may be occupied with the blessed heavenly things that are ours, and in our minds have left the wilderness and find ourselves in what answers to Canaan.

We are blessed with all spiritual blessings in heavenly places in Christ. We are chosen to be holy and without blame before the Father of our Lord Jesus Christ. We have received the adoption of children by Jesus Christ. Here is a sphere of thought and feeling outside of this world of time and sense. As another [J. N. Darby] has said, "We are introduced into a life which is *on the other side of death* by the power of the Spirit of God, as being dead and risen in Christ, there must be the remembrance of that death, by which we have been delivered from that which is *on this side of it*, of the ruin of man as he now is, and of the fallen creation to which he belongs."

Canaan cannot be the full type of Heaven for there was stern fighting for the possession of Canaan, and there will be no fighting in Heaven. It links on with Ephesians. "We wrestle not against flesh and blood, but against principalities, against powers, against the rulers of the darkness of this world, against spiritual wickedness in high [*heavenly, same word as in* Ephesians 1:3] places" (Ephesians 6:12). We are exhorted to take the whole armour of God that we may be able to stand, and not give up this wonderful portion that is ours.

In the type when the children of Israel passed over the Jordan, the river of death, the first movement was upon the part of the priests bearing the Ark of the Covenant. A space of 2,000 cubits had to be between it and the people. They had not passed that way heretofore.

As soon as the feet of the priests were dipped in the brim of the river, the waters of Jordan rose and stood up in a heap, very far from the city Adam, that is beside Zaretan, and those, that were flowing to the Dead Sea, failed and were cut off, and the people passed over.

Many have tried to explain this miracle as resulting from a landslide up stream that dammed the waters. But this cannot be. Jordan at that time of harvest had overflowed all its banks. And it was not till the priests' feet were dipped in the brim of the river that the miracle happened.

Note the Ark of the Covenant had to go first. Our Lord had to die. He bore the storm, He went through the tempest. He sank in deep waters. Alone He went into death, so that when we come to the river of death, we may find no water in it, but pass over dryshod.

> *"He passed through death's dark raging flood*
> *To make our rest secure."*

What a triumph is ours!

As soon as the priests' feet touched the brim of the river, the flood of waters ceased. As soon as all had passed over and the priests' feet were lifted up to the dry land, the waters returned.

Instructions were given that twelve men, a man from each of the twelve tribes of Israel, were each to carry a stone on his shoulder from the very place where the priests' feet had stood when they bore the Ark of the Covenant into the midst of the river bed, and then bring these twelve stones to the place where they were to lodge that night.

When any Israelite should ask in the days to come what was the meaning of the stones, this was to be the answer, "That the waters of Jordan were cut off before the Ark of the Covenant of the LORD; when it passed over Jordan, the waters of Jordan were cut off: and these stones shall be for a memorial unto the children of Israel for ever" (Joshua 4:7).

This typically tells us that even when we are in the Heavenlies in our spirits, tasting those things which will be ours in all their fullness in Heaven itself, when we have our glorified bodies, and are with our Lord and like Him, that God would not allow us to forget where the foundation of our blessing was laid.

I remember going up to the top of a New York skyscraper many years ago. When we got to the dizzy height, I said to my friends as I looked over the parapet, "I never felt the necessity of a good foundation as I do to-day." They replied, "The foundation of this building consists of four stories beneath the level of the street, ribbed in steel, and exceedingly strong."

And so when we get to the heights of Christian experience on the other side, the Spirit of God will not allow us to forget the atoning death of our Lord, the foundation on which is built all our blessing.

Is there not a charming intimation of this when we read in the description of the holy Jerusalem, the symbolic city setting forth the Church in administration during the Millennium, "Come hither, I will show thee the Bride, the *Lamb's* wife?" In that gorgeous scene we read, "The Lord God Almighty and the *Lamb* are the Temple of it", and again, "The *Lamb* is the light thereof"; and again, "a pure river of water of life, clear as crystal, proceeding out of the throne of God and of the *Lamb*"; finally we read, "The throne of God and of the *Lamb* shall be in it" (Revelation 21:9, 22-23; 22:1, 3). The *Lamb* speaks of sacrifice, "Behold, the *Lamb* of God, which taketh away the sin of the world" (John 1:29).

We shall never forget our Lord as *the Lamb of God* throughout eternity.

Joshua finally took twelve stones, and embedded them in the midst of Jordan, where the priests' feet had stood whilst the people passed over. Thus was typified the fact that all that we are in the flesh is gone in the death of Christ, so that finally in the ways of God only *new* creation, *new* life, will stand before Him.

Chapter 25:
Melchizedek, Type of Christ as Priest and King upon His Throne

READ GENESIS 14:17-24; PSALM 110; HEBREWS 7

We have thought it well to add this chapter, as there is a link between our Lord as the Priest after the order of Melchizedek, and His carrying out of His priesthood after the Aaronic order, as set forth in the Epistle to the Hebrews.

A good deal of controversy has arisen over the mysterious figure of Melchizedek. Some think he was Christ Himself, but this could not be, for he was "made like unto the Son of God". Some treat him as a real man, whose history afforded types that set forth our Lord. Others think he was a special creation of God, but that could not be, for a special creation of God would have a beginning of days. Others think he was a man, who was born, lived and died, but of whom there was no record of his birth or death, and with this we agree.

The best plan is to examine the Scriptures that bear on the subject, and let them speak for themselves.

In Genesis 14 we read that four kings made war with five neighbouring kings in the neighbourhood of the Dead Sea. The four kings triumphed over the five, and in taking the goods of Sodom and Gomorrah they captured Lot, Abram's nephew, who dwelt in Sodom, and his goods, and departed. The news of this was taken to Abram, who acted promptly, armed his trained servants born in his house, pursued the kings unto Dan in the far north of the country, made a night attack, and recovered his nephew Lot and his goods, and his women, and the people.

On returning Melchizedek met him with bread and wine, and blessed him saying, "Blessed be Abram of the Most High God, possessor of Heaven and earth; and blessed be the Most High God, which hast delivered thine enemies into thy hand" (Genesis 14:19-20). Thus suddenly and mysteriously appeared Melchizedek upon the scene. We are told three things about him in Hebrews 7. His name means King of righteousness. He was King of Salem, which means King of Peace, and further he was a priest of the Most High God. He was a King and a Priest. Mark well, his double position.

Abram paid him tithes. That was equivalent to homage due to a king from a subject. Tithes mean that the person to whom they are rendered has the right to the whole, just as God has the right to all that we have, and yet graciously accepts what we render to Him. King David in his day in the thankfulness of his heart exclaimed, "For ALL things come of Thee, and *of Thine own* have we given Thee" (1 Chronicles 29:14). One hundred per cent comes from Him, even if we render to Him a tenth.

Melchizedek is at once marked out as a wonderful person when Abram paid such homage to him. He distributed to

Abram bread and wine. Anticipating somewhat, Melchizedek typifies our Lord when He shall take up Israel again in the last days. The war between four kings against five is typical of the battle of the nations in the last days when our Lord, like Abram, will interfere and deliver His ancient people from their enemies, and distribute bread and wine to them and the world. They are talking of "a new world order", but that cannot come till the Prince of Peace comes to reign, the true King of Salem. Bread speaks of *sustenance*, and wine speaks of *joy*. Sustenance and joy under such a King will mean the Millennium.

The Jewish nation rejected their Messiah. Little did they recognize that the One they rejected was their Messiah, and as far as the Jewish nation is concerned He has gone into the Holiest of All, and until *He comes out*, Israel waits for her time of blessing. When our Lord does appear He will appear in the Melchizedek character. What a day will that be for this poor sin-stained world, soaked in tears and sodden with blood!

Further in Hebrews 7 we are told that Christ could not be a priest after the Aaronic order, for that order came of the tribe of Levi, and our Lord came of the tribe of Judah. But is our Lord not to be a priest? Yes, a priest after the order of Melchizedek. As King He came of the Davidic, the kingly family, and as King He will represent God to the people. As Priest He will represent the people to God. He will be both King and Priest on His throne.

Then the Apostle Paul argued that Melchizedek was greater than Levi, because when Abram paid tithes, Levi was still in his loins, as Scripture phrases it. If Melchizedek received such homage from Abram, Abram thus acknowledging his greatness, then Levi his descendent would have to pay similar homage.

Moreover, perfection was not found under the Levitical priesthood, their High Priest was made "after the law of a carnal commandment" so a change in the priesthood was necessary, that One after the similitude of Melchizedek should arise, who is made "after the power of an endless life" (Hebrews 7:16).

Note, there was no High Priest in the Melchizedek order, for there was only one Priest in that order. This mysterious figure suddenly arising in Genesis 14, passes off the scene, and as far as any notice is taken, there is no record of his birth or his death. Thus he finds his Antitype in the blessed Son of God, our Lord Jesus Christ. Brief as the description of Melchizedek is in Genesis 14 he was the most remarkable type of our Lord in all time. Hebrews 7 fills in details which are not found in Genesis 14.

First he was the priest of the Most High God. This is a Millennial title of our Lord, pointing to the time when He will take His rightful place with Israel as King and Priest upon His throne, His throne and priesthood covering the whole world, for "if the casting away of them be the reconciling of the world, what shall the receiving of them be, but life from the dead?" (Romans 11:15). "When the Most High [Hebrew, *Elyon*] divided to the nations their inheritance, when He separated the sons of Adam, He set the bounds of the people according to the number of the children of Israel" (Deuteronomy 32:8). "That men may know that Thou, whose name is JEHOVAH, art the Most High [Hebrew, *Elyon*] over all the earth" (Psalm 83:18). When the Lord takes His place over the earth, it means the Millennium.

This is borne out by the name, Melchizedek, which means *King of righteousness*, whilst his title, King of Salem, means *King of peace*. This is a grand combination, which will be seen in the Antitype, our blessed Lord, in a future day in full result. This world is needing righteousness and peace badly. Every problem solved righteously and peace reigning, what a world that will be, a world that poets have dreamed of, and sung, which politicians have striven after, but all hitherto has been failure, for

THE CENTRAL FIGURE,

Christ, has been left out. What good is the rim and the spokes of a wheel, if the hub is left out? There can be no wheel without a hub, and there can be no "new world order" without Christ. There cannot be a circumference without a centre.

And further we come to the very foundation of these titles. How can there be peace without righteousness? That is an impossibility with God. Thank God, Christ has settled the whole question of sin *righteously* at the cross of Calvary when He made atonement for sin. Peace now can be proclaimed, and whilst all believers share now in this righteousness and peace, one day these will visit this sad earth, and joy and gladness will come.

> *"He'll bid the whole creation smile,*
> *And hush its groan."*

Next we have a most important statement. It says of Melchizedek, "Without father, without mother, without descent, having neither beginning of days, nor end of life; but made like unto the Son of God; abideth a priest continually" (Hebrews 7:3). Adam was without father and mother, and without descent, but he had beginning of days and end of life, so he is ruled out. The priests could not claim the Aaronic priesthood unless they could trace their descent from Aaron, and unless they could claim both father and mother to be of the Aaronic line. Or, if we take it in its very literal meaning, it could not refer to the Lord as to His Manhood, for as Man He had a mother, and had beginning of days, and end of life. Therefore it refers to our Lord as THE SON OF GOD, in other words as the Eternal Son. Of no one could it be said but of Deity, that He has neither beginning of days nor end of life. That postulates Deity, and nothing short of that. We have no doubt, but that Melchizedek was born, and lived, and died, but evidently in a time of the world's history when a man's parentage was carefully recorded, and his birth and death as carefully noted, but here was a man whom none knew when he was born, nor when he died, in other words he appeared as having neither beginning of days, nor end of life. The great testimony given to him is that he LIVED.

He was "made like unto the Son of God". Then the Son of God existed before Melchizedek was made like to Him. What a proof of the Son as *eternal* in the unity of the Godhead—Father, Son and Spirit, one God, inscrutable but most blessed mystery, filling the heart of the believer with adoring worship.

At the present moment our Lord is acting with Aaronic functions for His people, and in this way Aaron is typical of Him as we have seen repeatedly in the former chapters. But the day for Israel and the world is coming, when He will come out as of the Melchizedek order, the one and only true Melchizedek, and bless Israel and the world at large. That day is surely drawing nigh.

Zechariah gives a glowing prophecy as to this. We read, "Behold the Man, whose name is THE BRANCH; and He shall grow up out of His place, and He shall build the

Temple of the LORD; even He shall build the Temple of the LORD; and He shall bear the glory, and shall sit and rule upon His throne; and He shall be a Priest upon His throne; and the counsel of peace shall be between them both" (Zechariah 6:12-13). Note our Lord will be

A King upon His throne.
A Priest upon His throne.

Kingship and Priesthood will unite in one blessed Person. Of course it was necessary for our Lord to become Man in order to die an atoning death upon the cross of Calvary. But in the end the world will rejoice in the advent of the eternal Son of God in the character of the true Melchizedek, a Priest and King, ushering in peace and plenty and joy, bringing in bread and wine, bread to sustain and wine to give joy. Then will come the true new world order.

Chapter 26:
The Seven Feasts of the Lord

READ LEVITICUS 23

It has been said that till a Christian can explain the seven Feasts of the Lord, the seven parables of the Kingdom of Heaven, and the seven addresses to the Churches in Asia as found in Revelation 2 and 3, he has not got very far in Christian knowledge [Dr W. T. P. Wolston].

There is no doubt these three sevens cover an enormous extent of truth. Our object in this chapter is to look a little at the Seven Feasts of the Lord.

Leviticus 23 begins by emphasizing that man must work six days, and that the seventh—the Sabbath—is a day of rest, but verse 4 says emphatically as to what follows, "*These* are the Feasts of the LORD", and from that point seven are specified. They are:—

1. *The Passover.*
2. *The Feast of Unleavened Bread.*
3. *The Feast of Firstfruits.*
4. *The Feast of Pentecost.*
5. *The Feast of Trumpets.*
6. *The Great Day of Atonement.*
7. *The Feast of Tabernacles.*

Some commentators think that the Sabbath is the first of the seven Feasts, and treat the Passover and the Feast of Unleavened Bread as one, thus still counting the seven Feasts of the Lord.

But on looking at the beginning of Leviticus 23 this exposition does not seem to be justified. Verse 3 emphasizes the Sabbath, the day of rest. But verse 4 says, "These are the feasts of the LORD", and then proceeds to enumerate the seven Feasts of the Lord.

Why then should the Sabbath have such a prominent place to begin with? The answer is that the Sabbath typifies *the very end of God's ways in grace on earth*, even His own entrance into the rest He has had ever before Him, of accomplishing all the purposes of His grace and love to men. The very word Sabbath [Hebrew, *Shabbath*] means *cessation of work*. "He spake in a certain place of the seventh day on this wise, And God did rest the seventh day from all His works" (Hebrews 4:4). The Sabbath typifies the eternity of rest that lies before God when He will rest in the complacency of His love, when righteousness shall dwell. "We, according to His promise, look for new heavens and a new earth *wherein dwelleth righteousness*" (2 Peter 3:13).

In short we have here an example of God setting the end before us, and then giving us the Feasts of the Lord, as showing how He works in grace with Israel and His Church to His goal of glory and eternal rest.

Then further the Sabbath is never called by itself a Feast, though there are Feast days that specifically occur on the Sabbath. Finally the Sabbath was a *weekly* occurrence, whilst the Seven Feasts of the Lord occurred *annually*. It would have thrown things out of gear to have a feast occurring fifty-two times in the year, and the others annually, as one set of feasts. Verse 4 settles the point, "*These are the feasts of the* LORD".

These seven Feasts of the Lord were celebrated as follows:

The Passover . . . . 14th day of 1st month
The Feast of Unleavened Bread . . . . 15th-21st day of 1st month
The Feast of Firstfruits (Harvest time) . . 16th day of 1st month
The Feast of Pentecost, fifty days later . . 6th day of 3rd month
The Feast of Trumpets . . . . 1st day of 7th month
The Great Day of Atonement . . . . 10th day of 7th month
The Feast of Tabernacles . . . . 15th day of 7th month

These break up into *three* sections. The first *two* set forth God's way of dealing with man, the foundation of all His ways in grace, whether in Old Testament or New Testament times, whether with Jew or Gentile.

The *third* and *fourth* set forth this present dispensation, marked by neither Jew nor Gentile, but the Church of God.

The *fifth, sixth*, and *seventh* set forth God's dealing with the Jews after the Church is raptured to glory.

Thus we reach the very end of God's ways in grace, and come to the threshold of the Eternal State, the Antitype of the Sabbath.

Let us now take these up in detail.

THE FEAST OF THE PASSOVER

The Passover was the beginning of God's dealing with Israel in establishing relationship with Himself. They must be a *redeemed* people at the outset. This was typical. But we are left in no doubt as to what it typified. We read, "Christ our Passover is sacrificed for us" (1 Corinthians 5:7), Christ's sacrifice is actual and efficacious on behalf of the believing sinner.

How often has the Passover night in Egypt been enlarged upon by the gospel preacher, so that we need not say much about it here. How often have we rejoiced over this Scripture, "And the blood shall be *to you* for a token upon the houses where ye are: and when *I see* the blood, I will pass over you, and the plague shall not be upon you to destroy you, when I smite the land of Egypt" (Exodus 12:13). God sees the blood, typical of the precious blood of Christ, this satisfies Him as to His righteous claims and His holiness, and that *same* blood is given to the believer as the token for his *assurance*. What more could we have? As the hymn puts it,

> *"God is satisfied with Jesus,*
> *I am satisfied as well."*

If God is satisfied, the believer may well be.

Acquaintance with God on the ground of redemption as the foundation of God's ways in grace, is typically presented to us in the Passover, when we read, "This month shall be unto you the *beginning* of months; it shall be the *first* month of the year to you" (Exodus 12:2). It *started* the Jewish calendar, and typically testified that God could only begin relationship with His people on the ground of redemption.

THE FEAST OF UNLEAVENED BREAD

If the blood of the Passover gave TITLE to God to redeem His people, and bring them with a strong and out-stretched hand from the land of their bondage, the Feast of Unleavened Bread sets forth that there must be MORAL SUITABILITY on the part of the people, if they were to be happy with God. They must be a sanctified people.

This feast flowed out from the Passover as its consequence, but though it immediately followed, it will be seen how different they were. The Passover was God act-ing typically in righteous grace in relation to His people on the ground of redemption. The Feast of the Unleavened Bread was the answer that God expects from His people in their practical ways on earth. Leaven had to be put out of their dwellings; that is, evil has to be refused on their part.

We get the connection between the two feasts in the New Testament, where it says, "Christ our Passover is sacrificed for us; THEREFORE let us keep the feast, not with old leaven, neither with the leaven of malice and wickedness; but with the unleavened bread of sincerity and truth" (1 Corinthians 5:7-8).

Christ is our Passover. Brought to God on the ground of redemption, holiness becomes those who stand in rela-tionship with God. Evil, typified by leaven, has to be excluded from our lives. "Follow ... holiness, without which no man shall see the Lord" (Hebrews 12:14). These words are addressed to believers, to each one of us.

The Feast of Unleavened Bread lasting seven days typifies our whole responsible life down here, the eighth day lead-ing to the day, which has no evening and morning, the eternal Sabbath of God's rest, the eternal State when God shall be all in all.

THE FEAST OF FIRSTFRUITS

Verse 9 of our chapter, with the opening sentence, "And the LORD spake unto Moses", marks a new section, intro-ducing us to the Feast of the Firstfruits and the Feast of Pentecost.

These two feasts are marked very significantly by the for-mula, "On the morrow after the Sabbath" (verse 11) and "unto the morrow after the seventh Sabbath" (verse 16).

The Sabbath is the great day connected with Judaism. They were accustomed for all their feasts more or less to circle round the Sabbath. What could this new departure mean, "the day after the Sabbath"? The answer is that the "day after the Sabbath", that is "the first day of the week", *is connected with* CHRISTIANITY. To this hour the unbelieving Jews celebrate their Sabbath every seventh day of the week, whilst "upon the first day of the week … the disciples came together to break bread" (Acts 20:7) as their custom was in apostolic times, a custom in the mercy of God permitted to us to this present time.

In short we may ask, What great event occurred on the first day of the week? The answer is, The most wonderful moment in the history of this world was when our Lord, the triumphant Conqueror over sin and death and hell, rose from the dead. So it is no wonder that the first day of the week was called the Lord's Day. The apostle John wrote, "I was in the Spirit on the Lord's Day" (Revelation 1:10). It was indeed a very special day.

The Jew's rejection of Christ brought in a new era, that of Christianity. A Jew who gets converted to-day drops Judaism religiously, and embraces Christianity. And until the Church is raptured to glory it will be true that "blindness in part is happened to Israel, until the fulness of the Gentiles be come in" (Romans 11:25).

So these two Feasts, the Feasts of the Firstfruits, and the Feast of Pentecost, must have occasioned much enquiry in Old Testament times, but when we come to the New Testament, we get the key to it very plainly, as we shall see.

The harvest in nature is used as a type of the harvest in grace. Our Lord, as He noted the people of Samaria streaming out in response to the woman's invitation, "Come, see a Man, which told me all things that ever I did: is not this the Christ?" (John 4:29), said to His disciples, "Say not ye, There are yet four months and then cometh harvest? behold, I say unto you, Lift up your eyes, and look on the fields, for they are white already to harvest. And he that reapeth receiveth wages, and gathereth fruit unto life eternal: that both he that soweth and he that reapeth may rejoice together" (John 4:35-36).

When the Jewish harvest in the field was to be reaped, a Sheaf of the Firstfruits was brought unto the priest, and his office was to wave it before the LORD "on the morrow after the Sabbath".

This is clearly a type of Christ *in resurrection*. He lay in the tomb all the Sabbath, surely showing that there was no blessing according to the law and for Israel on those lines. In that great resurrection chapter, 1 Corinthians 15, we read, "Now is Christ risen from the dead, and become the FIRSTFRUITS of them that slept" (verse 20). Again we read in the same chapter, "As in Adam all die, even so in Christ shall all be made alive. But every man in his own order: CHRIST THE FIRSTFRUITS; afterward they that are Christ's at His coming" (verses 22-23). So this great New Testament resurrection chapter clearly links up with Leviticus 23.

When it says, "*In Christ* shall all be made alive", this does not teach, as the universalists do, who deny eternal punishment, that all mankind shall be eventually saved. All mankind is not "in Christ". Born into this world, the offspring of a fallen race, we are all "in Adam". To be "in Christ" means to be saved, to be a believer on the Lord as Saviour. Christians can look back to a moment in their history when they put their faith in the Lord and passed from death unto life. The Apostle Paul in his salutation to the Church of God in Rome wrote, "Salute Andronicus and Junia, my kinsmen, and my fellow prisoners ... who also were IN CHRIST *before me*" (Romans 16:7), showing these relations of the Apostle had been converted at a time when he was unconverted.

Another point to be observed is of all importance, in that the very word, FIRSTFRUITS, typically shows that it is a sample *of the whole harvest of grace*, of which all believers form a part. How our blessing is all wrapped up for confirmation in the resurrection of Christ is seen in the argument, "If Christ be not raised, your faith is vain; ye are yet in your sins" (1 Corinthians 15:17).

In this connection Romans 8:11 is a very illuminating Scripture. We read, "If the Spirit of Him that raised up Jesus from the dead dwell in you, He that raised up Christ from the dead shall also quicken your mortal bodies by His Spirit that dwelleth in you." Note the wonderful connection. Christ was raised by the power of the Holy Spirit. That same Holy Spirit has been sent by an ascended Christ in glory to indwell each believer as the *pledge* that just as HE *was raised*, so shall saints on the earth, alive when the Lord comes, be quickened as far as their mortal bodies are concerned by that same Spirit. The Spirit is given as the *seal*, or the pledge of this. Christ was raised *representatively* just as He died *representatively*, and His resurrection carried with it the promise and pledge of the resurrection of all God's people, who have fallen asleep in Jesus, or, if alive on the earth, their bodies will be quickened into bodies of glory like our Lord's.

In connection with the waving of the Sheaf of the Firstfruits, a Burnt Offering—a lamb without blemish—was offered up, typifying God's delight in all the sweet savour to Him of the sacrifice of Christ.

Note there was NO *Sin Offering*, as there was with the new Meat Offering as we shall see presently. There could be no Sin Offering as applying to the Lord personally.

A Meat Offering was also to be presented to the Lord, a Drink Offering accompanying the same, typifying God's delight in the devoted life of our Lord even unto death, and the joy—the Drink Offering—connected with it. Neither bread, nor parched corn, nor green ears were to be eaten till the Offering was presented to God, thus emphasizing that nothing can be enjoyed spiritually till the foundation of all has been laid in the death of Christ, and until we begin with Him.

THE FEAST OF PENTECOST

The Feast of Pentecost was to be celebrated on "the morrow after the seventh Sabbath", with its special meaning of "the first day of the week", the great day of this Christian dispensation, as the Sabbath was of Judaism. Moreover it was to take place *fifty* days after the Wave Sheaf was waved before the Lord.

What great event happened fifty days after Christ rose from the dead? The very word, Pentecost [Greek, *Pentecoste*, means fiftieth], points to that great happening described in Acts 2:1-13. We know how our Lord remained on this earth forty days after His resurrection, and before His ascension. The disciples were to tarry at Jerusalem until they were "endued with power from on high" (Luke 24:49). "And when the day of Pentecost [*the fiftieth day*] was fully come, they were all with one accord in one place. And suddenly there came a sound from Heaven as of a rushing mighty wind, and it filled all the house where they were sitting. And there appeared unto them cloven tongues like as of fire, and it sat upon each of them. And they were all filled with the Holy Ghost, and

began to speak with other tongues, as the Spirit gave them utterance" (Acts 2:1-4).

On the day of Pentecost, "the morrow after the Sabbath", "the first day of the week", fifty days after our Lord rose from the dead, the great event took place of the bestowal of the Holy Spirit to be in this world as He had never been before. Indwelling each believer, it was the glorious day of the Church's birth. On that day the Church was constituted. The mystery hid from all ages emerged in the sight of a triumphant Head in Heaven, even our Lord Jesus Christ, and believers on earth were indwelt by the Holy Spirit of God, thus linking each believer with the Head in Heaven, and with each other as members of the one Body on earth. "There is one Body, and one Spirit, even as ye are called in one hope of your calling" (Ephesians 4:4). "Christ also loved the Church, and gave Himself for it; that He might sanctify and cleanse it with the washing of water by the Word, that He might present it to Himself a glorious Church, not having spot or wrinkle, or any such thing; but that it should be holy and without blemish" (Ephesians 5:25-27).

Thus clearly can we see that the "*New* Meat Offering" is typical of the Church of God upon this earth. Indeed there is no such clear intimation of the Church upon earth in the Old Testament pages, as we find in Leviticus 23. At the same time the relation between the Head in Heaven and the members of the one Body on earth could not be hinted at in Old Testament times. This constituted "the mystery which hath been hid from ages and from generations, but now is made manifest to His saints" (Colossians 1:26).

THE NEW MEAT OFFERING

The New Meat Offering consisted of *two* loaves. The two loaves set forth how Jew and Gentile believers are bound together in this new and blessed association. Nothing less than this wonderful truth would make the Jew forget that he was a Jew religiously, or the Gentile that he was a Gentile "afar off", and in the warmth and glory of the conception of the Church in its relation to the Head in Heaven forget their long-time religious feud, than which none could be more bitter. This is a word that is needed to-day. The Church of God oversteps all frontiers, differences of language, differences in social position, colour of skin, and makes one all believers on the face of the earth in one blessed Christian fellowship. There is ever the tendency to limit the Church in one's mind to the country to which we belong, or the small section of Christians with whom we may walk.

This is all guarded against in Ephesians 2:13-14. We read, "Now in Christ Jesus ye who sometimes were far off [*Gentiles*] are made nigh by the blood of Christ. For He is our peace, who hath made both [*Jew and Gentile*] one, and hath broken down the middle wall of partition between us [*Jew and Gentile*]." How good it is when all walls of partition are broken down in the mighty flow of divine love, and by the living influence of the Holy Spirit of God.

These two loaves were to be of fine flour *baken with leaven*. Why leaven? In Leviticus 2:11 we are told "Ye shall burn no leaven, nor any honey, in any offering of the LORD made by fire." This seems to contradict this instruction to burn no leaven in any offering made by fire. It is true that in every case without exception where the Offering sets forth CHRIST *personally* no leaven is allowed.

It would be unthinkable to speak of leaven, or evil, in connection with Him.

But this is a *New* Meat Offering, not the Meat Offering (Leviticus 2) setting forth Christ personally, but one that sets forth the Church as the product of the death of Christ. This *New* Meat Offering does NOT, however, set forth *Christ personally*, but the *Church* composed of Jew and Gentile, who both before their coming into blessing were sinners, and who, even as saints, might sin. The leaven in the Offering acknowledged that. The fact that it was baken in the oven sets forth that the working of the leaven would be arrested by the fire. And furthermore in addition to a Burnt Offering, and a Meat Offering with its attendant Drink Offering, there was a SIN OFFERING and a Peace Offering. This offering is carefully described as the *New* Meat Offering.

We remember in the Feast of the Firstfruits, typically setting forth Christ in resurrection, there were a Burnt Offering and a Meat Offering with its attendant Drink Offering, but NO SIN OFFERING. How could there be a Sin Offering when the feast set forth *our Lord personally?* But in this case the Sin Offering answers to the leaven in the fine flour of the loaves, acknowledging what had been the character of the saints before conversion. Even in this New Meat Offering there were these sacrifices accompanying it, that show that the Church can only be looked upon as an offering to the Lord as the believers approach in all the efficacy of the work of Christ, whether seen in the Burnt Offering, the Meat Offering, the Sin Offering, the Peace Offering, and that such approach covers all these particular types of the death of Christ.

THE GLEANING OF THE HARVEST

Leviticus 23:22 is a very remarkable verse. There shines from it the clear light of Divine inspiration. We read, "And when ye reap the harvest of your land, thou shalt not make clean riddance of the corners of thy field when thou reapest, neither shalt thou gather any gleaning of thy harvest: thou shalt leave them unto the poor, and to the stranger: I am the LORD your God." Note where this verse lies. It is situated between the *New* Meat Offering Feast, typical of this present dispensation of God's grace in connection with His Church upon this earth, and the Feast of Trumpets; that bringing in the last three Feasts that pertain to God's dealing with the Jews, His own people and the nations, after the Church is raptured to glory.

This verse sets forth that when the Harvest of this present dispensation is over as the result of the preaching of the Gospel of the grace of God, there will be a special movement of God's Holy Spirit in reaching the Jews with the Gospel of the Kingdom to prepare them for their reception of their Messiah and King, the Lord Jesus Christ. Through the Jews the message will go out to the poor and the stranger—the heathen nations of the world—in preparation for the day when the Lord shall reign as universal Lord as the Son of Man and "the earth shall be filled with the knowledge of the glory of the LORD, as the waters cover the sea" (Habakkuk 2:14).

Not many details are given in Scripture as to this. Perhaps the fullest and clearest is found in Matthew 25:31-46, which tells us of the Lord's earthly brethren, Jewish evangelists, preaching among the nations in view of the day when the nations shall be gathered before the judgment seat of Christ. The sheep, those receiving the Gospel of the Kingdom, will be separated from the goats, those who reject this testimony—the sheep to pass into life eternal, that is into millennial blessing, and the goats into everlasting punishment.

It is interesting that sheep and goats are always found mixed together in the flocks of Palestinian shepherds, and the separation of the sheep from the goats would be a vivid way of presenting what will take place in the last days.

THE FEAST OF TRUMPETS

With the New Meat Offering we leave the Christian dispensation, typified in this interesting chapter. Again we get the formula, "And the LORD spake unto Moses". We come now to God taking up the Jews for blessing, to implement His promises to Abraham and to give His Son His earthly rights as the Messiah and King over Israel, and over the wide world as Son of Man. "Ask of Me, and I shall give Thee the heathen for Thine inheritance, and the uttermost parts of the earth for Thy possession" (Psalm 2:8).

We read, "Speak unto the children of Israel, saying, in the seventh month, in the first day of the month, shall ye have a Sabbath, a memorial of blowing of trumpets, an holy convocation" (Leviticus 23:24). A trumpet, a loud sounding instrument, that played a large part in the signals for the moving of the camp from time to time, symbolizes some arresting movement of God's Holy Spirit in connection with the revival of God's earthly people after their long centuries of unbelief and the judicial blindness that has overtaken them. In the words of Scripture, "Blindness in part is happened to Israel, until the fulness of the Gentiles be come in" (Romans 11:25). Zechariah, too, throws light on this subject for he predicts the day will come when there will be a Divine outpouring "upon the house of David, and upon the inhabitants of Jerusalem, the spirit of grace and of supplications: and they shall look upon Me whom they have pierced, and they shall mourn for Him, as one mourneth for his only son, and shall be in bitterness for Him, as one that is in bitterness for his firstborn" (Zechariah 12:10).

It is a remarkable sign of the times that the Jews have been returning to their ancient land in large numbers, going back as predicted in the Old Testament Scriptures in unbelief, all telling the tale that things are developing in preparation for this wonderful Feast of Trumpets when it comes. It will be so arresting that there will be no mistake about it. But there is no doubt that the extraordinary way the Jew is returning to his own land, and all the developments that are happening as the result of this, is all foreshadowing the time when the Feast of Trumpets will take place.

THE GREAT DAY OF ATONEMENT

Ten days after the Feast of Trumpets the Great Day of Atonement was celebrated. When the spirit of grace and of supplications are poured out by Divine goodness on the Jewish nation, when they shall look on Him whom they have pierced, then the nation will experience a deep spirit of humiliation, so deep that husband and wife will humble themselves *apart*. All classes will take part in this. We read, "The family of the house of David apart, and their wives apart [the *kingly* family]; the family of the house of Nathan apart, and their wives apart [the *prophetic* family]; the family of the house of Levi apart, and their wives apart [the *priestly* family]; the family of Shimei (see Numbers 3:18) apart, and their wives apart [the *Levitical* family]" (Zechariah 12:12-13).

226

In such a spirit of deep humiliation the nation will celebrate the Great Day of Atonement as it has never been celebrated before. It will be such a celebration as will betoken the acceptance of their Messiah, and that the One they have long rejected is their true Messiah, whose work at the cross, and the shedding of His precious blood, is the glorious fulfilment of all the types and shadows. The Jews revere these shadows, but so far have missed their true meaning as connected with the One they have despised and rejected. What a glorious day that will be for the world, the introduction of a true "new world order" founded on righteousness, peace and security through the personal reign of our Lord on the earth. We read, "If the casting away of them [*viz. the Jewish nation governmentally*] be the reconciling of the world, what shall the receiving of them be, but life from the dead?" (Romans 11:15).

THE FEAST OF TABERNACLES

Fifteen days after the Feast of Trumpets, and five days after the Great Day of Atonement, the Feast of Tabernacles took place. This Feast is typical of the Millennium, the thousand years' reign of Christ on this earth. It is the wind-up of God's dealings with Israel on the earth. It is interesting that prophecy concerning the Jew never goes beyond the Millennium. See Isaiah 65, where it speaks of "new heavens and a new earth" (verse 17), but it goes on to speak of Jerusalem *on earth*, it speaks of a sinner being accursed, showing plainly that Isaiah prophesied of an earthly time, even the Millennial reign of our Lord. But when we come to the New Testament prophecy goes further. When the earth and heaven have fled away, the very scene of the Millennium gone, there will appear "a new heaven and a new earth" (Revelation 21:1), wherein righteousness shall dwell, when there will be no more tears, sorrow, crying, pain or death. We shall be in eternity then in the full meaning of that word.

During the Feast of Tabernacles, which took place at the end of the Harvest, a time of plenty and rejoicing, a faint picture of the fulfilment of the type in the days to come, the Israelites by birth were to dwell in booths to remind them how God had brought them out of the land of Egypt. They might forget this in the comfort of the land and in the joy of the bountiful reign of their Messiah with all its accompaniments of peace and plenty never before known in the world. It does not do for us to forget the pit out of which we have been dug, that we are after all, with all the wondrous blessings that are ours, sinners saved by grace.

NUMBERS 29

Numbers 29 is a remarkable chapter. Its setting occurs when Israel had got out of the wilderness, and had arrived in the land on the east side of the river Jordan. In this chapter we are given fuller details than anywhere else as to the offerings that were required in connection with these three Feasts of the Lord, viz., the Feast of Trumpets, the Great Day of Atonement, and the Feast of Tabernacles.

One remark may be made about the offerings made on the eight days of the Feast of Tabernacles. On the first day among other sacrifices, *thirteen* young bullocks were offered up as a Burnt Offering. The next day they sacrificed *twelve*, and day by day the number was diminished till on the seventh day only *seven* bullocks were offered. Does this not set forth how everything committed to man has the tendency to lose its first enthusiasm? Ephesus lost its first love. The last times were viewed in the lifetime of the Apostle Paul. Many antichrists were seen in John's day. The seven churches addressed in Revelation 2 and 3 end with Laodicea, which was only fit to be spued out of the mouth of the Lord.

The Millennium has got two sides to it. First it hails the triumph of our Lord Jesus Christ. He gets His rights as David's heir and reigns over His ancient people. "They shall all know Me [the LORD] from the least of them unto the greatest" (Jeremiah 31:34).

On the other hand it will be the last and greatest test of man, and here it shows how incorrigible fallen mankind is under ideal circumstances. Surely after such a reign there should be nothing but holy submission to God's will. Nay, as soon as the personal hand of the Lord is withdrawn, we find, when Satan is loosed from his imprisonment in the bottomless pit during the thousand years' reign of Christ, that he will go out to deceive the nations, and under his awful leadership there shall be seen the last and biggest revolt against God that has ever been. In untold numbers they will spread over the earth, and attack Jerusalem, called "The beloved city". Fire will come down from God, the last revolt will be over. See Revelation 20:7-10. The earth and the heavens shall pass away, the elements shall melt with fervent heat, the earth and all its works shall be burned up, and "we, according to His promise, look for new heavens and a new earth, wherein dwelleth right-eousness" (2 Peter 3:13). Such is the man in the flesh that even the personal reign of Christ does not alter him.

But shall God be defeated? By no means. We read, "then cometh the end, when He [*the Son*] shall have delivered up the kingdom to God, even the Father; when He shall have put down all rule and all authority and power. For He must reign, till He hath put all enemies under His feet. The last enemy that shall be destroyed is death" (1 Corinthians 15:24-26). In one word the eternal state will be a scene where every trace of sin and sorrow, and man's will, will be absent, a scene marked by "GOD ... ALL IN ALL" (1 Corinthians 15:28).

We rise up from our task with two very deep impressions, made so by cumulative testimony to these two things as we considered the Tabernacle's Typical Teaching. The first impression is that there can be no having to do with a holy God, no way of blessing for the sinner, save through the atoning sacrifice of our Lord Jesus Christ, and through that alone. The necessity for this, the solemnity of it, cannot be exaggerated. The second impression is that along with the perfect standing of the believer on the ground of the atoning sacrifice of Christ, there is the insistence again and again of the necessity of moral suitability, if we have to do with God.

The two deep impressions circle round the truth set forth by the symbolic meaning of the blood and the water. They can be compressed into two verses:—

"The blood of Jesus Christ His Son cleanseth us from all sin" (1 John 1:7).

"Follow ... holiness, without which no man shall see the Lord" (Hebrews 12:14).

Any weakening of either of these two great facts is fraught with very evil consequences.

Appendix: Notes

CHAPTER 1: THE COLLECTION OF MATERIALS FOR THE CONSTRUCTION OF THE TABERNACLE, AND THEIR TYPICAL MEANING

[1] Estimates in the text are based on a price of silver of about 5 shillings (£0.25) per ounce, and a gold price of some 16 times this.

As of early 2009 the price of silver is around £8.64 per troy ounce, and the price of gold is around £569 per troy ounce, about 65 times this.

[2] 1s. 1½d. equates to 5.625p (£0.05625) in present UK currency; i.e. just over 5½p. At the 2009 value of silver, this would be approximately £1.90.

CHAPTER 3: THINGS WORTHY OF NOTE IN CONNECTION WITH THE TABERNACLE AND ITS SERVICE

[3] *1 cubit:* 1 foot 9.888 inches (55.595 cm)

1 shekel (silver): 2s. 3.37d. [11.4p] (at 5s. [25p] an ounce); at 2009 value, just under £4.

1 talent of silver (3,000 shekels): over £11,000 at 2009 value.

1 talent of gold (approximately 16 x value of silver historically; approximately 65 x value of silver in 2009). So 1 gold talent would be worth over £750,000 at 2009 prices.

CHAPTER 5: THE TABLE OF SHEWBREAD

[4] *viz.*: Latin, A contraction of the term *videlicet*, meaning "namely" or "that is to say".

CHAPTER 6: THE GOLDEN CANDLESTICK

[5] *114 lb:* 114 troy pounds is equivalent to 93.8 pounds or 42.55 kg (see also notes [3] and [8]).

CHAPTER 8: THE BOARDS OF THE TABERNACLE

[6] *17 feet high and 2½ feet wide:* 5.18 metres high and 0.76 metres wide.

[7] *1s. 2d.*: more accurately, 1s. 1½d. = 5.625p (see [2] above).

[8] *"A talent of silver weighed 114 lbs., which at 5s. an ounce amounts to over £340, so that the two sockets allotted to one board would mean silver to the value of £680. The 100 sockets for the fifty boards amounted to the sum of about £34,000."*: there are 12 troy ounces in a troy pound, so 114 troy pounds is 1368 troy ounces, which at 5s. (£0.25) per troy ounce is £342. Thus it appears from this part of the text that troy weights (as used for the measurement of precious metals) are being used. The 2009 value would be over £11,810 per socket, giving a total of almost £1,182,000 for the 100 sockets.

CHAPTER 11: THE COURT OF THE TABERNACLE

[9] *twenty shillings in the pound:* that is, "the full amount".

Chapter 13: The Consecration of Aaron and His Sons

[10] *condign:* "well-deserved and appropriate".

Chapter 22: The Cleansing of the Leper

[11] *leprosy:* Since the book was first written, treatments for the modern condition of leprosy (Hansen's disease) have become available, with varying degrees of success. The disease is still widespread: some 254,525 newly detected cases outside Europe were reported to the World Health Organization for 2007. The reader should bear in mind that the Biblical condition called "leprosy" in many translations describes a wider range of conditions than Hansen's disease alone.

[12] *log:* approximately 1 pint (½ litre).

OTHER BOOKS FROM SCRIPTURE TRUTH PUBLICATIONS
UNDERSTANDING THE OLD TESTAMENT SERIES:

HOW TO OVERCOME BY JOHN T MAWSON
ISBN 978-0-901860-62-0 (paperback)
144 pages; April 2009

DELIVERING GRACE BY JOHN T MAWSON
ISBN 978-0-901860-64-4 (paperback)
ISBN 978-0-901860-78-1 (hardback)
192 pages; March 2007

ELIJAH: A PROPHET OF THE LORD BY HAMILTON SMITH
ISBN 978-0-901860-68-2; (paperback)
80 pages; March 2007

ELISHA: THE MAN OF GOD BY HAMILTON SMITH
ISBN 978-0-901860-79-8; (paperback)
92 pages; March 2007

THE GOSPEL IN JOB BY YANNICK FORD
ISBN 978-0-901860-76-7 (paperback)
ISBN 978-0-901860-77-4 (hardback)
112 pages; March 2007

LESSONS FROM EZRA BY TED MURRAY
ISBN 978-0-901860-75-0 (paperback)
84 pages; March 2007

LESSONS FROM NEHEMIAH BY TED MURRAY
ISBN 978-0-901860-86-6 (paperback)
124 pages; August 2008

234

UNDERSTANDING CHRISTIANITY SERIES:

SEEK YE FIRST BY JOHN S BLACKBURN
  ISBN 978-0-901860-61-3 (paperback)
  ISBN 978-0-901860-02-6 (hardback)
  136 pages; February 2007

GOD AND RELATIONSHIPS BY COR BRUINS
  ISBN 978-0-901860-36-1 (paperback)
  108 pages; August 2006

"THE EPISTLE OF CHRIST" EDITED BY F. B. HOLE
  ISBN 978-0-901860-73-6 (paperback)
  140 pages; March 2008

SHORT PAPERS ON THE CHURCH BY HAMILTON SMITH
  ISBN 978-0-901860-80-4; (paperback)
  96 pages; March 2008

GOD'S INSPIRATION OF THE SCRIPTURES BY WILLIAM KELLY
  ISBN 978-0-901860-51-4 (paperback)
  ISBN 978-0-901860-56-9 (hardback)
  484 pages; March 2007

LECTURES ON THE CHURCH OF GOD BY WILLIAM KELLY
  ISBN 978-0-901860-50-7 (paperback)
  244 pages; February 2007
  ISBN 978-0-901860-55-2 (hardback)
  244 pages; March 2007